REMAKING FLORHAM

FROM GILDED AGE ESTATE TO CAMPUS OF FAIRLEIGH DICKINSON UNIVERSITY

Carol Bere
Walter Cummins
Eleanor Friedl
Harry Keyishian
Arthur T. Vanderbilt II

FLORHAM BOOKS

Remaking Florham: From Gilded Age Estate to Modern College Campus

Prepared by Carol Bere, Walter Cummins, Eleanor Friedl, Harry Keyishian, and Arthur T. Vanderbilt II

Copyright © 2019

ISBN: 978-0-578-42823-9

Published by Florham Books

First Florham Books Edition 2019

The great majority of photographs are from the Fairleigh Dickinson University archives. Content sources include Peter Sammartino's *I Dreamed a College* (A. S. Barnes, 1977), *Samuel A. Pratt: The First Decade of Campus Development (1999)*, and contributions by students from the campus' initial years.

CONTENTS

Remaking Florham is the fourth in a series of books on the history of the Vanderbilt–Twombly estate. The first, *Florham: An American Treasure*, provides an overview from the decision to create the estate to its present role as a university campus. The second, *Joseph Donon: The Richest and Most Famous Private Chef in the World*, tells the story of the man who provided gourmet French cuisine for the Twomblys for almost forty years and who was a major influence on twentieth century fine dining. The third, *Olmsted's Vision: The Landscape of Florham*, describes the role of the man who created the tradition of landscape architecture in the United States as he and his followers designed the landscaping and gardens of the Florham estate.

Remaking Florham

We owe the existence of the Florham Campus of Fairleigh Dickinson University to a set of coincidences. In the mid-1950s, with the growth of its Rutherford and Teaneck, New Jersey, campuses, the University was seeking land for potential expansion into Morris County. During the same period, in 1954, Ruth Twombly, the daughter of Florence Vanderbilt Twombly, who had a major role in managing the estate, died two years after her mother. The surviving daughter, Florence Twombly Burden, and her family did not want to maintain ownership.

The great majority of the estate's approximately 1,000 acres—primarily the Florham Farm—was purchased in 1955 by ESSO (later EXXON) for what became a complex of administrative and research facilities. That left close to two hundred acres of the residential area—the Mansion, Carriage House, Playhouse, Orangerie, and many smaller buildings—up for sale.

Florham as an Estate

Florham was one of the many Vanderbilt mansions, homes designed by the greatest architects of the time and decorated and furnished with valuables from around the world. Vanderbilt family members, similar to other society members of the Gilded Age, generally had two or three residences: a townhouse in New York City, a country estate, and a seaside "cottage" located in Newport, Rhode Island.

Florence Vanderbilt Twombly and her husband, Hamilton Twombly, chose Morris County, New Jersey, for the site of their country home because of its proximity to New York City and, more significantly, because of the area's appeal to many of their social class already living on nearby estates and in neighboring mansions. By the turn of the twentieth century, the Morristown area was being referred to in newspaper articles as "the Millionaire City of the Nation."

The estate buildings, including the Mansion, were designed by famed architects McKim, Mead & White, and included many outbuildings such as an orangerie, greenhouses, a carriage house, and a gatehouse. The Mansion, its design influenced by that of the Christopher Wren wing of Hampton Court Palace in England, was ready for occupancy by the Twomblys in 1897.

The total cost of the Mansion itself was reported as $700,000 at the time. This figure excluded such interior embellishments as the Barberini tapestries. Adding in the cost of such items and others like landscaping—raised the total price of the house to perhaps $2 million. The entire estate with its gardens, farm, and outbuildings may have required an outlay of approximately $5 million at the time.

Frederick Law Olmsted, Sr., the country's leading landscape architect, and his firm were responsible for the design of Florham's grounds—the trees, shrubbery, and initial gardens. Olmsted himself was involved initially, first convincing Hamilton Twombly to build the estate, and then establishing the basis of the planning carried out by his successors.

The University had been considering property farther west in Morris County in the town of Chester. Instead, the real estate agent who had been showing homes in the area to the chairman of the University Board of Trustees, Edward T. Williams, introduced him to the possibilities of Florham. Williams and other Board members convinced the University's founding president, Peter Sammartino, to make the purchase. And the campus was born, opening for classes in 1958.

Today, it is called the Florham Campus. At the beginning, it was called the Madison Campus because of its mailing address, even though all but one of the existing buildings were in the Borough of Florham Park. Then it became known as the Florham-Madison Campus and later, for several years, the College at Florham.

The transition from estate to campus presented a challenge to adapt facilities and infrastructure. What had been rooms for guests and entertaining had to be made suitable for academic purposes. Electricity, plumbing, and access had to serve the needs of hundreds rather than dozens. Even so, the process was completed relatively quickly and smoothly in just months.

The name Florham signifies the strong continuity between the estate and the campus. Despite a number of new buildings and residence halls and the daily presence of many students, a visitor may still experience the ambiance of a time when the McKim, Mead & White-designed building and the Frederick Law Olmsted-inspired landscaping and gardens were the home to a mother and daughter and the one hundred servants and grounds workers who maintained their way of life.

Florham had been an estate from 1897 to 1955. It has been a campus even longer, from 1958 to the present, with an enduring commitment to preserving the heritage of the past.

The End of the Estate

With the deaths of Florence Vanderbilt Twombly in 1952 at the age of ninety-eight, and her daughter, Ruth, in 1954 at the age of sixty-nine, the curtain essentially came down on Florham, and a way of life that would probably never be replicated. The fate of Florham was not unique in the area or in the country. In fact, Florham had survived and prospered for many years after similar estates had failed.

The Gilded Age of luxury began to dissipate in the 1930s for a variety of reasons: the effects of the imposition of the personal income tax; the financial collapse of 1929 with its related effects on all areas of the economy (and personal lives); the lack of concerted preservation efforts; and also the natural gravitation of people to other areas. Beginning in the l930s, shifts in the Morris County area followed this pattern as many of the great homes neighboring Florham along Madison Avenue and in surrounding areas, began to be demolished, while over the years some were occasionally retrofitted for other purposes.

Florence Twombly had left an estate of $22 million, but taxes reduced this figure to slightly more than $18 million. After payment of legacies, there were not enough funds to honor planned bequests to hospitals and churches.

A single event that signified the end of the Vanderbilt Twombly way of life was the two-day auction conducted in the mansion by Parke-Bernet Galleries on June 15 and 16, 1955. The contents of Florham were up for sale.

Among the objects auctioned were a variety of Renaissance, Chippendale, Georgian and Dutch furniture, Oriental and Persian carpets, oil paintings, valuable 18th-century English colored mezzotints, period chandeliers, decorative objects such as carved jades and Chinese porcelain, and legendary tapestries. Complete bedroom accoutrements including Georgian-carved mahogany bedsteads, matching dressers, bedspreads, and window "treatments" were also on the auction block.

While the almost 600 objects put up for auction could provide an exemplary case study of the Gilded Age, the size and scale of most of the furnishings dictated that many homes could not accommodate these pieces, with the result that a fair number were sold at far lower prices than the appraised value.

Total sales of the auction of Florham furnishings and other "appointments" came to $141,415. Along with $200,000 from an earlier auction in New York in January 1955, the total came to $341,415. Translated into present-day figures, the Vanderbilt Twombly estate sale would have been $2.5 million.

There's little doubt that a "sense of an ending" motivated the many people—curious local residents, window-shoppers, wealthy socialites, and determined dealers—who swarmed the grounds and mansion of Florham, which was open to the public for the first time since the turn of the century for a two-day previewing of what was arguably one of the finest collections of furnishings of its time. And what the viewers saw, perhaps even momentarily experienced, was a slice of history.

Arthur T. Vanderbilt II describes the scene in his book *Fortune's Children: The Fall of the House of Vanderbilt*: "Thirteen thousand sightseers from five states parked along the two-mile drive to the house and on the lawns, come to see how life had once been lived in the Gilded Age. As dealers hurried from room to room, turning over vases, examining paintings with magnifying glasses, measuring rugs, the curious sat down in chairs covered in silk brocade and felt the tapestries. They turned the solid silver knobs on the mahogany doors, tried out the bell system that once had summoned the servants, and wandered through the gardens and around the grounds, peering into the Orangerie, the playhouse, the stables. Who could resist a peek at how life had once been?"

A panoramic picture of the estate on the days of the auction was written by Brendan Gill for *The New Yorker* in 1955: "Florham," he wrote, "is everything one thinks an English country seat should be, with the greenest of green lawns running on into groves of oak and beech, and, rising against the sky at the end of a long graveled drive, a hundred-room house of rosy brick, its roof bristling with chimneys, its many doors open to the summer air." He noted "the dainty palace of an orangerie, all arched windows and glint of glass … the charming crisscross of gardens and paved walks, of pavilions, pergolas, urns on pedestals and grave Greek statues."

After the auction, the Twombly heirs slashed the annual expenses of running Florham from $250,000 to $90,000, still, in 1955, an enormous sum and enough to keep a small army of workers to maintain it as the great estate was put on the market. Although the heirs of Florence and Ruth Twombly chose not to keep Florham, the estate was still maintained by the family—albeit not on the original grand scale—until the sale of Florham in 1957.

In 1957, Esso Research & Engineering Company bought 685 acres where the farms had been for $2 million. Plans for an ESSO research campus were approved in May 1957. Some 1500 truckloads of materials from the demolished farm buildings were hauled away, some of which was given to the Morristown Airport for use as fill for new runways. The first Esso employees moved to the site on Labor Day weekend in 1959. Besides three large office buildings, another twelve—pilot plant, laboratory, and utility buildings were built there over the years.

The fate of the residential portion of the estate, 183 acres, lay in uncertainty. Would the grand buildings be demolished, the elegant landscape destroyed? Plans swirled about for subdivisions in Florham Park that would include 900 homes, shopping centers, schools, public utilities, and garden apartments. To avoid a housing development that would have added 8,000 residents and placed great pressures on the town where all but a small part of the estate lay, Florham Park rezoned the property for industrial use and subdivided it. The neighboring town of Madison was given 42 acres for a high school by the Twombly heirs and grandsons, Shirley and William A. M. Burden.

When Fairleigh Dickinson University agreed to purchase the property, the town avoided a crisis, and a campus was born.

The Purchase of the Campus

In his very personal book, *I Dreamed a College*, Peter Sammartino, founder and first President of Fairleigh Dickinson University, explains the acquisition and development of the land and buildings of the Florham estate in 1957 to create the University's third New Jersey campus, now called the Florham Campus.

In the mid-1950s, although the University was flourishing with its two campuses in Rutherford and Teaneck, President Sammartino recognized the need for more space in the future as New Jersey was changing with new developments and new industries. The University did move to purchase 200 acres in Chester for agricultural purposes in light of Sammartino's keen interest in nutrition and organic foods. The farming plan, however, did not materialize.

In the spring of 1957, the chairman of the Board of Trustees, Edward Williams, was seeking a home in Madison to be closer to his office in the newly merged Warner Lambert Company in Morris Plains. Williams also mentioned to his realtor that he was looking for a "large open space for a possible school." The realtor showed him Florham.

Although President Sammartino thought the property to be "too rich for our blood," with assurances from the Board that funds for the purchase of the property were available and the terms attractive, the acquisition of Florham became final in August 1957.

Hi Blauvelt, one of the trustees, has fallen in love with the place. While I was away [in Maine] he worked on the owners, who had bought it from the Twombly estate, and he got them to lower the price by $500,000. He also got them to spread the payments over a seventeen-year period.

—Peter Sammartino

President Sammartino writes of bringing a group of administrators and faculty for their first view of the campus: "After riding through a beautifully kept road and underneath a railroad trestle, a magnificent building came into view, reminiscent of Hampton Court in England. As we reached the impressive courtyard, I stopped. Sally [Sammartino's wife] and I got out and the rest followed suit. "Well," I said, "this place is ours. Now what in hell do we do with it?"

The task troubled Sammartino: "It [the Mansion] was hardly ideal for university purposes. It was discouraging even to contemplate turning this ornate palace into a smoothly running school."

He worried about the complexity of the grounds, the capacity of the heating system and the lighting, the old-fashioned plumbing, the water system, the fact that the sewage system depended on septic tanks, and the cost of maintaining "the magnificent estate."

Yet buildings and rooms were renovated for academic use, and the campus opened in the fall of 1958.

The Conversion to a Campus

Under the University, the Twombly mansion took on the formal name of the Mansion. The building today contains administrative and faculty offices, classrooms, meeting rooms, and the Twomblys' Drawing Room, renamed Lenfell Hall in honor of University benefactors Leonard and Felicia Dreyfuss, as a setting for large gatherings such as formal dinners, lectures, concerts, and other events. In 2007, the Mansion was renamed Hennessy Hall after alumnus and former Board of Trustees chairman, Edward L. Hennessy, Jr.

During the initial years of the campus, the Mansion contained the library and student dormitory rooms. Eventually, over several decades, a library was added behind the Orangerie, more residence halls were constructed, classroom buildings added, as well as a student center and a recreation center with a gymnasium, weight rooms, and a competition swimming pool. More than 1,500 students now live on campus.

When the campus opened, the conversion of estate rooms and building for academic purposes used Florham's original structures. In the next fifty years, many changes were made with the construction of new facilities, including a library and residence halls. The function of rooms in the Mansion itself has undergone several reallocations.

In 1958, however, on the first floor, Miss Twombly's office (9) became the Dean's office; the Drawing Room (2), a Convocation Hall; the Billiard Room (11), the Trustee's Room; the Family Breakfast Room (14) the Admissions Office; the Dining Room (7) a classroom; the Library (6) and Reception Room (5), both library rooms; the Cloak Room (8), the switchboard.

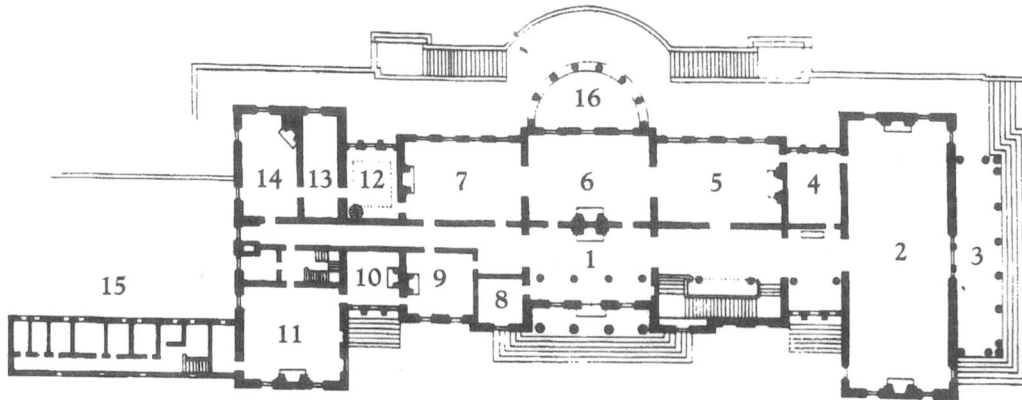

The family quarters in the south wing of the second floor and the guest rooms on that floor, all became classrooms. The guest rooms and baths of the third floor, along with servants' quarters in the north wing, became a women's dormitory. The male servants' quarters on the ground floor north wing became the men's dormitory.

The basement kitchen and food storage area served as the college cafeteria, and the maids' and male servants' sitting rooms became the student commons.

The Carriage House was turned into a science building with eleven laboratories. Ruth Twombly's Playhouse became the college gymnasium, and the indoor tennis courts became a basketball court.

The Acquisition of Florham: Peter Sammartino

In his book I Dreamed a College *(1977), Peter Sammartino, the founding President of Fairleigh Dickinson University, describes how the University came to purchase the campus, and the challenges faced in converting an estate to a college campus, as well as his own misgivings about the project.*

I now had had experiences with two campuses and I realized two things that I didn't fully appreciate when I started in the old castle in Rutherford: 1) an institution really never knows how much land it needs; and 2) communities change, and what may look like a very good location at the start may be much less attractive within fifty years. Eleven acres in Rutherford seemed like a lot of space in the forties; thirty-five in Teaneck didn't seem so much in the fifties. New Jersey was changing so fast. New upper-middle-class towns sprang up almost overnight; bustling textile industries died and faded out of sight, creating urban blight. Some colleges were becoming uneasy in carefully guarded enclaves in depressed areas. So far we were lucky in Rutherford and in Teaneck. Our campuses were open to the town.

A MAGNIFICENT BUILDING CAME INTO VIEW

It is true that in Rutherford the avalanche of cars had produced a difficult situation, but we had solved that by spreading out the cars, and as new owners of houses came in they tended to acclimate themselves to the existing state of affairs. After all, the town citizens themselves were adding to the problem. There were old houses of the era when there were no garages, which now had four cars in the driveway. But in each of the two towns the college was a stabilizing force, an entity that lent an intellectual aspect to the community, a place to show off to visiting friends. Some colleges are walled in—as our Florham-Madison campus was to be. The Rutherford and Teaneck campuses melted into their towns. But now, I began to feel that we should purchase about two-hundred acres in less-populated areas and put them aside for the far future when none of us would be around.

I had already started on this idea but for a different reason. I had always been interested in nutrition and natural or organically grown food. I had begun to realize in the late forties that it was going to become more and more difficult to secure pure foods for the students. I was naïve enough to think that we could grow our own vegetables for institutional use. I had gotten a friend of mine, June Burn, to look for a farm in a twenty- or thirty-mile circle—with no results. As we extended the area of search, she found a sleeper—the 250-acre estate of a Polish contractor (who had died intestate) for which the state was receiving bids. I told her to bid 300 an acre. Feeling sure we would never

Drive to the Mansion in the 1950s

get it, I soon forgot all about the matter as other pressing problems engulfed us. Then, all of a sudden, by coincidence as J.I. Rodale, the founder of *Prevention* magazine, was having lunch with me, the reporters burst upon me wanting to know what we proposed to do with the property we had purchased in Chester, New Jersey. Was there going to be a new campus? Evidently, the state had accepted our bid and announced it to the press without bothering to inform us first. I spluttered a few feeble phrases, but what was worse was that the trustees, including my own father-in-law, were miffed that I had purchased this tract without the formality of obtaining trustee approval. Actually, all I had done was to enter a bid and of this I had kept them informed. For once, I was caugnt off-guard and, to this day, Dick Dickinson probably still thinks I acted precipitously. The matter did come up at the next trustees' meeting and my action was approved in regular fashion.

With the help of my friend, Dr. Ehrenfried Pfeiffer, the authority on biodynamic farming, we started in bravely by first planting cover crops and plowing them under to enrich the soil, by creating rich compost heaps, and by bringing in thousands of June bugs and earthworms. But it soon became evident that it was impossible to get farm help. We tried custom or contract farming, but this too turned out not to be feasible. At any rate, we had enough acreage to meet the needs of a new campus fifty or sixty years hence.

By chance, a new set of circumstances was evolving almost simultaneously. The chairman of our board lived in Ridgewood, New Jersey. He had a long, irksome trip to the new factory of the newly merged Warner Lambert Company in Morris Plains. He called in a realtor and asked him to find a new home in the Madison area. As an afterthought, he said to him, "Oh, by the way, if you find a few-hundred acres for sale, and suitable for a school, let me know." This was in accord with the suggestion I had made. (Chester hadn't been in the picture at that time.) Some time later, the realtor found a home for Ed Williams; he also found 157 acres of prime land, but with some of the most beautiful residential buildings in America.

It was in the spring of 1957 that Ed took me to see the estate. I was impressed with it but I expressed the opinion that it was too rich for our blood. The matter was discussed at the May meeting of the board, but in deference to my reluctance no motion to purchase was presented. So I went to Maine with a great load off my mind. But I hadn't heard the last of it. Hi Blauvelt, one of the trustees, had fallen in love with the place. While I was away he worked on the owners, who had bought it from the Twombly estate, and he got them to lower the price by $500,000. He also got them to spread the payments over a seventeen-year period. This they were glad to do, because taxwise it was to their interest. Ed Williams was not hard to sway; neither were some of the other trustees. The scene shifted to Maine. Bill and Annette Schieffelin were having dinner with us at East Sullivan, Maine. The phone rang. It was Ed Williams. Usually he was very direct and forceful. This time his voice was hesitant and almost apologetic.

Board of Fellows members tour the new campus

"Peter, if you don't have to worry about the financial part of it and if you can delay using the property for as long as you wish, would you still have objections to acquiring Florham?" he asked.

"Ed," I replied, "what can I say? I sense that the trustees want to acquire this estate."

I returned to the table and mentioned the matter to Bill. "Florham?" he exclaimed, "Why, Mrs. Twombly was my great-aunt! Annette and I used to spend many happy weekends there."

15

He then proceeded to tell us of the society at the turn of the century that frequented the estate known as Florham, which was used only in the spring and fall because the Twomblys had a winter home in New York City and a summer residence in Newport, Rhode Island. Every Friday afternoon, thirty or forty guests would arrive at Florham for the weekend. Each couple usually would be assigned a suite. Joseph Donon, the major domo, with a staff of chefs, would work all week to prepare the weekend meals, each one of which would be a Lucullan feast. This then was the property that had been acquired by the college. This was mid-August, 1957.

The call had spoiled the sweetest part of my vacation in Maine. I had to come down to sweltering Rutherford for a special meeting I had called of seventeen administrators and key faculty men. The flash call probably spoiled things for them, too. They met at my home at eight in the morning and naturally wanted to know what all the mystery was about. "Just get into your cars and follow me," I replied. They followed me to Madison Avenue in Madison, New Jersey, long known as the Rose City of America. Finally, after passing the College of St. Elizabeth, we came to a beautifully bricked wall, and when we saw two massive pillars we pulled into two open iron gates. After riding through a beauti- **THIS PLACE IS OURS. NOW WHAT IN** fully kept road and underneath a railroad trestle, a **HELL DO WE DO WITH IT?** magnificent building came into view, reminiscent of Hampton Court in England. As we reached the impressive courtyard, I stopped. Sally and I got out and the rest followed suit.

"Well," I said, "this place is ours. Now what in hell do we do with it?" There was a low whistle, a gasp of incredulity, and then the questions began to tumble forth.

Slowly, I told them the full story. This was the estate known as Florham, built by Mr. and Mrs. Hamilton McK. Twombly. Florence Twombly was the granddaughter of Commodore Cornelius Vanderbilt. Hamilton Twombly was a partner of J. Pierpont Morgan. Florence and Hamilton Twombly had built the estate, one of the most beautiful in America, and the name Florham came from Florence and Hamilton. They had spent millions on the palace, two million on the grounds alone, and this at a time when gardeners were getting a dollar a day. They had built another edifice for their daughter Ruth. Since she liked tennis, it had the most expensive clay court in America, plus a dazzling indoor swimming pool with frescoed walls, surrounded by exotic trees and shrubs. Most abandoned estates look abandoned. This one did not. Every blade of grass had been carefully cut. The marble halls within the palace were glistening. The massive mahogany doors had been French-polished by hand. Most of the bathrooms had luxurious dressing rooms attached.

We sat on the grand stairway, because there was no furniture in the place, and all morning we discussed the various alternatives that faced us. In general, the question was: should we just not do anything for two or three years, or should we start using this place immediately? What courses and curricula should we have on this campus if we were going to use it? How many students should we prepare for? We had lunch, we returned, and we voted on the question. The vote was unanimously in favor of immediate opening; that is to say, an opening as soon as the campus could become ready. Whereupon we proceeded to look into other matters. Their reasoning was sound. They felt that since the estate had been maintained so beautifully, both as far as the buildings and as far as the grounds were concerned, we might just as well plunge into a new campus rather than lose this great advantage. That is how Florham-Madison became the third campus of Fairleigh Dickinson University.

Since this was in the summer of 1957, we would naturally have to wait until September 1958 to open up. Before another week had gone by, we had or-

IT WAS DISCOURAGING dered laboratory equipment. I approached the building of a new campus at Madison with a heavy heart. While it was true that the estate with its magnificent mansion was one of the great showplaces of the nation, to me it represented an almost insuperable operational problem. First, having gone through the process of building up two campuses from run-down estates, I was not eager to go through another such experience, even though Florham had been kept up in tip-top condition. Second, I had fallen in love with contemporary architecture. With increasing costs of maintenance and operations, I felt that contemporary architecture with its clean-cut lines and functional efficiency was the only answer to good institutional operation. But once one trains one's eye to contemporary lines, everything else becomes old hat. The fact that the mansion at Florham had been copied from Hampton Court did not register with me at all. It was a handsome Georgian building; it was nostalgic. So what? It had been built as a private home. It was hardly ideal for university purposes. It was discouraging even to contemplate turning this ornate palace into a smoothly running school. Third, the complexity of the grounds really worried me. The heating plant had never been intended for winter living, since the Twomblys lived in New York during the winter. The plumbing was old-fashioned—the pull-chain type of the turn of the century. The lighting was distinctly toned down for subdued living and was never meant for mass reading needs. The sewage system depended on septic tanks. It was all right for family living—completely inadequate for institutional use.

Actually, the soil tests showed that the ground was poor for an institutional sewage system. The use of detergents presented a grave danger to the water supply. Modern detergents tend to break down the soil, resulting in sewage seepage into the water supply. As a matter of fact, this is exactly what is happening in some towns. I tried to find out from some of the larger manufacturers what could be done about the problem. The replies were evasive and made me realize all the more the seriousness of the situation. It almost seemed at a certain point that we would have to give up the campus entirely because of the sewage impasse. Fortunately, at this very time a nearby town was setting up a sewer authority, with which we could hook up; even though the cost was higher than we had envisaged, it was the best, the safest, and really the unavoidable solution for our problem. This factor of cost was to torment us in Madison from the very beginning. I never wanted a third campus, as I have said so many times in public,

I NEVER WANTED A THIRD CAMPUS

and today if l had to make the decision, I still would not have it. But, I am practically alone in this point of view. I didn't want a third campus because with our slim resources it meant spreading what we had over three instead of two campuses. It meant also that we would have to parcel out our creative energy and this under difficult circumstances. Madison was almost an hour's travel away. A trip to Madison meant a day away from the office. It was difficult for me; it was equally difficult for the administrators and faculty members from other campuses who had to travel there. Later, the Madison people found it equally difficult to attend meetings at the other two campuses.

All who came to the new campus were struck with the beauty of the lawns, the trees, and the shrubs. The mansion is a prize example of Georgian architecture. But it cost money to keep up this magnificent estate, money that we had to siphon off from badly needed things at the other campuses. In a letter to the trustees, I had compared what was happening to a man who argues with his wife about badly needed curtains for the kitchen while he lavished a mink coat on a floozie on Park Avenue. Everything was now there, Ed Williams argued: the roads, the sewers, the water supply. But was it? The roads, five miles of them, were built for a maximum of forty or fifty cars a week for twenty weeks a year. Now we would have three-thousand cars and heavy supply trucks daily. The old roads soon had to be rebuilt. I've mentioned the sewers. Even the water supply provisions had to be enlarged at great expense. I was overwhelmed with the immensity of the place. I finally was able to contact Mr. Donon, who had been the major domo of the estate. As a French soldier, he had been severely wounded during World War I. When Mrs. Twombly asked Mrs. Frick, her next door (or next block) neighbor at Fifth Avenue and 71st Street, to recommend someone who could help her at Florham, Mr. Donon's name had been suggested. Curiously, Mr. Donon now owned the French paper, which through various mergers was *La Voix de France*, which I had owned until 1942 when I divested myself of that newspaper, plus a publishing concern, in order to concentrate on the founding of our new college. Little by little, with Mr. Donon's help, the endless succession of rooms and cavernous basements lost their awesome aspect. Fortunately, our architect, Roland Wank, was not only equal to the job; he was intrigued by it.

I was fortunate also in choosing one of our youngest additions to the faculty as the new dean for the campus, Dr. Samuel Pratt, whose wife, Lois, also had a doctorate in sociology. They made an ideal pair to help me

OVERWHELMED WITH THE IMMENSITY OF THE PLACE

organize the new campus. They had the energy of youth, they relished the challenge of starting a new institution, and they had imagination. This was the third old estate I had to turn into a college. I now had the dubious distinction of having to convert more old houses into collegiate institutions than anyone else in the history of higher education in America. We didn't want to do violence to the architectural and aesthetic ensemble. It represented the best that money could buy and we wanted to preserve the historical spirit that prevailed. Lighting was one of the greatest problems. While soft lights might be conducive to the social aspects of the Twombly era, they were ill-adapted to educational use. We had to change the lighting fixtures in the test classroom three times before we found an unobtrusive but efficient model that would not do violence to the style of the rooms. I even took a quick trip to Williamsburg to see how they had solved the problem in their Phi Beta Kappa building. When I observed their classrooms, I felt they had sacrificed too much to "atmosphere." I went to visit another college that had utilized a similar, if less grandiose estate, for college purposes. I was appalled at what I saw: a mélange of furniture, homemade, make-shift alterations, sloppiness everywhere, and poor maintenance.

Would our place look just as dilapidated?

But slowly we dug out from under. We solved the lighting question, the sewage problem, the institutional washrooms. We created good classrooms and good offices. We used the old orangerie as a front for our library, built a good annex to it, and gave carte blanche to the librarian as far as books were concerned. The old carriage house, which might house thirty or forty Rolls-Royces during the social weekends, became our science laboratory, and Professor Malcolm Sturchio did wonders in setting up facilities for physics, chemistry, and biology. I brought Dr. William E. Smith from the Sloan Kettering Institute to set up the Health Research Institute. The sheep barn became art studios, and the playhouse our gymnasium. It was a whirlwind year. We decided to have our June 1958 commencement at Madison just to familiarize people with the place. By that time (I still find it hard to believe it in retrospect), we had something WOULD OUR PLACE LOOK JUST AS DILAPIDATED? to show off even if everything had not been completed. But while the campus looked lovely, the commencement was marred by an invasion of seventeen-year locusts that had swarmed in the region. The insects kept dropping into the laps of parents resulting in occasional shrieks. They clustered around the microphone, their chirping made the speeches difficult to hear, and finally, as the audience marched out, it was to the squashing, ugly sensation of stepping upon hundreds of locusts. At any rate, the new campus was a functioning entity, in spite of the locusts.

We had a delicate problem in naming the new campus inasmuch as it straddled two towns, Florham Park and Madison. In order not to offend either community we decided on calling it Florham-Madison. Eventually, the name was too cumbersome and it became easier to refer to it as the Madison campus. The physical transformation of Florham-Madison from a residential estate into a college was just one part of the problem. The more important aspect concerned the educational aspects.

We started in Rutherford in 1942 with a two-year semi-professional college, but with a strong emphasis on a core curriculum of liberal-arts subjects. When, after six years, we became a four-year institution, the core curriculum remained intact but was expanded upward; that is, it became more advanced and widened its scope. When Teaneck was established, we maintained the emphasis on the liberal arts core curriculum, but we established two professional schools, which now had to bend to the dictates of the professional accrediting agencies. In Florham-Madison, our major aim was to develop it as a small liberal arts institution, with the original core curriculum prevailing. Now I had a special problem. I had to organize in the Morris County region, an area that was upper-middle class. In Rutherford we were serving a region that had few college facilities. In Florham Madison we were competing in a region where most of the high-school graduates were in the habit of going to college. We were also plunging into a city that contained Drew University and, in the adjoining town and abutting our campus, the College of St. Elizabeth. When the decision to buy the property had been made, as a matter of professional courtesy, I called Dr. Holloway and Sister Hildegarde Marie, presidents, respectively, of the two institutions. Both were away on vacation, and so the touchy chore had to be done by mail. I knew both presidents and I must say for the record that they both made us feel at home.

I established a new group of the Board of Educational Directors, principals of Morris County high schools, and met with them periodically, but at least twice a year in conjunction with the older group. There was a natural curiosity about the Twombly estate and, capitalizing on this, I was able to organize a group of outstanding citizens from the Morris County area to take an interest in our newest campus. Not the least important aspect of our new promotion was to point out to industries in the area the offerings and the opportunities for degree work at our evening college, and, indeed, we started in September 1958 with 652 evening students and 304 full-time day students. Again, we had created a new college in less than a year.

THERE WAS A NATURAL CURIOSITY ABOUT THE TWOMBLY ESTATE

At Madison, my educational philosophy was the same as before. I believed strongly in the importance of reading; hence, the emphasis upon a good, functional library. I believed equally strongly in inculcating the principles of good citizenship—understanding contemporary movements, intelligent participation in civic matters. This was to be effected through our social science core curriculum and out-of-class activities. I also believed in the importance of experiences of all sorts as complementary to the reading programs: laboratory, clinical projects, sociological surveys, trips, and field studies. I felt strongly about health, and indeed our first all-college visit was to an organic farm in Pennsylvania. All this was a bit more difficult to achieve. Everything in a college is nailed to the inflexible credit system. Activities beyond or in addition to courses tend to lose prestige. I believed in lifetime sports, and in Florham-Madison it was possible to emphasize these: tennis, swimming, golf, bowling, and dancing. I believed in the importance of people getting along with each other, within social groups, with members of their family, eventually with fellow workers. This kind of program demanded knowledge of psychology and philosophy, and they were added to the core curriculum. Since a knowledge of international affairs was essential in the contemporary world, I brought in outside speakers who had something to say in this area.

We were now a three-campus college, and since I wanted to learn how other multiple campuses were administered, I organized a two-day conference in New York and invited presidents who had more than one campus in the greater New York metropolitan area. We had no speeches, simply rapid-fire, across-the-table discussions of our experiences, of **THEY CONFUSED BROAD ACRES, MAGNIFICENT BUILDINGS, IDYLLIC SURROUNDINGS WITH ACADEMIC SUPERIORITY** basic philosophy, and of rational administration. We discussed faculty standards, faculty representation, student services, curricular offerings, library problems, admissions, evening sessions, and university calendars. We all profited by the exchange of ideas, and later on, inspired by this conference, I wrote a small volume on multiple campuses.

Now, a difference crept into our integrated existence—not during the first year, but slowly, within a few years. Florham-Madison was about an hour's ride from Rutherford or Teaneck, thus it was in a sense an isolated campus, isolated even from Madison itself. Teaneck and Rutherford overlapped, Florham-Madison didn't. It was off in left field, so to speak—but in a well-heeled left field. This was a campus of opulent pretensions reminiscent of an equally opulent past. No make-shift surplus buildings from Camp Shanks here. Gone was the humble stance of yesteryear.

And yet there was no new source of income. From the very first year, the campus began to carry its own weight operationally, but not from the point of view of capital expense, which had to be supplied by the other two campuses. At first the nucleus of faculty members came from the other two campuses who gave the new campus a sense of belonging to a family. But after the first year, the great proportion of the faculty consisted of new people and these had no similar sense of dedication. To them, Fairleigh Dickinson was Florham-Madison. Rutherford and Teaneck were the distant progenitors.

These new faculty members had no understanding of the blood, sweat, and tears that had made it possible for their campus to be born. They confused broad acres, magnificent buildings, idyllic surroundings with academic superiority. This was good in a way because it gave the new campus a sense of confidence, a feeling of instant excellence. It was bad in that it also induced a sense of jealousy at the other campuses. When we built the gymnasium in the playhouse in Florham-Madison, there was a feeling in Teaneck that it too should have a new gymnasium. To this day, Teaneck has had to make do with an old gymnasium. I didn't worry too much about it because to me, large gymnasiums are basketball-oriented—and mostly for audiences. The educational excellence of an institution does not depend on the size of a basketball audience, nor even on basketball itself. I take a dim view of intercollegiate competitive college sports.

At any rate, we had created another collegiate center in New Jersey. All who visited Florham-Madison were impressed by the beauty of the estate, and this naturally reflected on the University as a whole. It was an artificial and expensive way of building up our importance in the eyes of the national academic community, but such is the hypocrisy of life. As far as I was concerned, I would not have established a new campus; I would have concentrated on the two we had. But once the trustees had made their decision I worked as hard as possible to implement it.

IT WOULD BE A "DORMITORY" COLLEGE

But in spite of the logistics of travel, in spite of the natural divisiveness that occurs when the family gets larger, we did manage to have an overall cohesiveness that was *sui generis*. I had a student advisory group of fifty representatives from each campus who would meet with me periodically to discuss matters that concerned them: library arrangements, cafeteria provisions, dormitory rules, athletic events, and an assortment of petty gripes. I provided as many opportunities as possible for the faculty from the three campuses to meet, whether in the formal monthly meetings, university committees, or social functions. The administrative council met regularly with me. But I went a step further. I had always felt that the younger members of the faculty generally have little opportunity to present their point of view. So I organized a faculty advisory committee consisting of five members from each campus, elected by the junior faculty. Even the secretaries were drawn into the integrative pattern.

It was decided when we initiated the Florham-Madison campus that it would be a "dormitory" college. At first, the dormitory students slept on the third floor of the mansion. It took a few years before a large dormitory unit was erected. But I must point out that the only reason Florham-Madison was able to operate in the black was that we had a large number of commuting students, day and evening. Another project we tried was that of "Saturday Scholars" who could attend classes all day on Saturday and earn up to six academic credits. I tried to induce an esprit by having a communal lunch, but somehow it didn't work out very satisfactorily.

As we began to be known outside of New Jersey and also in many foreign countries because of our international activities, we received applications from prospective boarding students—that meant dormitories. But there was another matter occupying my mind. The State of New Jersey was creating far more institutions of higher learning than it really needed, if it took in consideration the capacities of its private colleges. The planning authorities were embarking upon a policy of creating a place for every high-school graduate who wanted to go to college. My own early survey of about two hundred New Jersey high schools showed that none of their graduates in the upper three-quarters had any trouble being admitted to college. A few, less than three hundred in the bottom quarter, did have some difficulty. It is true that about fifty-four percent of the high-school graduates went out of state, but this was because of the configuration of the state. Two-thirds of the college population was concentrated in the northeastern section, and this group could com-

MORE INSTITUTIONS OF HIGHER LEARNING THAN IT REALLY NEEDED

mute to thirty-seven colleges within a radius of an hour of travel across the state border or across the Hudson River. The other concentration was in the Camden-Philadelphia area, and this group could commute to twenty-six colleges, within an hour of travel, to colleges in Pennsylvania. Even in the Phillipsburg area, students could commute, nay walk, as former Governor Meyner did to Lafayette, to six colleges across the state line.

My survey also showed that eventually the fifty-four percent would go down within five years to forty-seven percent, but this was because of the community colleges, which would attract students who heretofore had not planned to go to college. As I write this, the percentage going out of state has gone down to forty-seven percent in spite of the hundreds of millions that have been spent for higher education colleges and in spite of sixteen new community colleges. People in New Jersey enjoy higher-than-average incomes. Their children can afford to go to college, and most young people like to go away to college—away from papa and mama. If you go one hundred miles in any direction except south, you're out of the state. In the south are only wastelands, although it now has more public institutions per capita than almost any part of the United States.

I was one of the few to see through the canard that there weren't enough places for college applicants in New Jersey. I realized that there would come a time when the competition of tax-supported institutions would draw many students away from us and that we would have to replace them with boarding students. We therefore made plans to build as many dormitories as we could on the three campuses in order to survive. Fortunately, the chairman of the board, Ed Williams, with whom I would discuss my fears and my prognostications, saw the future as I saw it and supported my move for maximum dormitory space.

Peter Sammartino

Peter Sammartino was a man of many accomplishments through his vision, his initiative, and his creativity. At the age of thirty-seven, and with his wife, Sally, he raised the backing to found a junior college in Rutherford, New Jersey, in 1942. Then, in 1948, he acquired the then-Bergen Community College as the University's Teaneck campus. The Florham-Madison campus opened ten years later. By the next year, 1959, total University enrollment had grown to almost 13,000 students.

Central to his inspiration was the realization that many World War Two veterans were eligible for the GI Bill that would finance higher education, and that the large population of New Jersey lacked sufficient colleges to accommodate them. The majority of these veterans were first-time college students preparing for roles in an expanding post-war economy with a need for people to fill managerial positions. That circumstance lay at the heart of Sammartino's educational philosophy. He himself was the son of a pastry chef from lower Manhattan.

Inspired by his experience as chairman of the language department at the New College, an experimental school at Columbia University's Teachers College, Sammartino affirmed that school's emphasis on hands-on learning. Students were expected to learn about real life by working in business, about social concerns by working in the community, and about global issues by studying abroad— groundbreaking notions at the time.

Describing his educational values, Sammartino wrote, "People think of a university in terms of buildings, of numbers of students, of complexity of curricula. And yet it was in terms of our service to students and the simplicity of our approach that we found the greatest meaning to our lives. This service, we felt, was by far the most important aspect of Fairleigh Dickinson. This was the magic web that held us together and gave us the élan that was the spirit of the institution."

Valuing international connections, he brought in students, faculty members and visiting lecturers from throughout the world. This commitment led to the purchase of Wroxton College in Oxfordshire, England, in 1965. Fairleigh Dickinson became the first American university to create an overseas campus. He also co-founded and served as the first president of the International Association of University Presidents, which today includes 700 presidents from around the world. The son of immigrants who entered this country through Ellis Island, he launched a nationwide movement and ultimately convinced Congress to provide funds to renovate the facility as a landmark.

While Sammartino's distance from the mainstream of American higher education freed him from the limitations of many preconceptions that might have constrained another man, it also led to a limitation as the University developed and its faculty wanted to become part of that mainstream. In 1967, the Trustees named him chairman and brought in a more traditional academic leader, J. Osborn Fuller, dean of liberal arts at Ohio State University, to fill the role of president.

Samuel A. Pratt

When Peter Sammartino chose Sam Pratt to direct the physical and academic creation of the University's new campus, he had as a bonus the participation of Pratt's wife, Lois, who also had a doctorate in sociology and significant academic experience. They shared much of the conceptualizing and planning for the campus.

Pratt earned degrees from the University of Connecticut, Michigan State University, and Harvard Business School, as well as his PhD from the University of Michigan. From 1952-58, he did extensive consulting and policy research for the federal government and for business. He also taught graduate courses in business administration at the University before becoming dean on February 21, 1958.

His duties as dean were multiple. He had to adapt the building and grounds for educational uses, hire the staff, and obtain basic services from area towns and businesses. He had to recruit faculty and schedule courses. He had to recruit students. He had to manage facilities and raise funds. And he had to develop relationships with local communities and the state.

Walter Savage, a founding faculty member, said, "Sam was—in addition to being resident carpenter, quartermaster, architect, labor-crew foreman, personnel director, public relations supervisor, curriculum planner, and faculty procurement officer, among other things—estate gardener."

Pratt was quite conscious of the fact that while the campus was part of a larger University, it was separated by distance from the other campuses and was located in an affluent area among industries that sought a well-educated work force. As a result, he believed the campus required a distinct academic identity, one in keeping with its setting on a magnificent estate.

Savage called Pratt's thinking "cutting edge" and noted that "His determination to make the Florham-Madison campus something altogther new alarmed several of his more traditionalist colleagues and superiors."

Influenced by the cultural changes of the 1960s, Pratt encouraged a number of new approaches to education. For example, returning from a meeting on new technologies, he confounded a classically educated English professor by predicting that students would replace writing with movie cameras, and that their use should be incorporated into many courses. That insight was decades ahead of its time.

Ultimately, Pratt's vision for the campus clashed with the educational philosophy of Peter Sammartino and, under pressure, he stepped down as dean for another position at the University, and soon moved on to an administrative role at another institution.

REDESIGNING ESTATE BUILDINGS FOR LEARNING

The objective of a university is to create as knowledgeable and as culturally sensitive people as we can, and one of the most important tools for doing this is a good physical plant. We're going to have a wonderful educational plant here.

Dr. Samuel Pratt

Creating Temporary Quarters

Florham's original buildings in Georgian style were designed for lavish living and entertaining. They needed to be adapted to accommodate the educational needs of the campus. The one hundred-room Mansion was modified to serve students, faculty, and administration as classrooms, offices, library, and bookstore. A student cafeteria and dormitory rooms were also set up in the Mansion and used until the new Twombly Hall residential building was completed. An 18-hole miniature golf course that had been laid out next to the "Playhouse" in 1924 by Mrs. Twombly for her athletic daughter was quickly put to use by students and faculty in the summer of 1958.

Student
cafeteria

Mansion conversion

Conversion of Mansion rooms

Twombly drawing room

converted to

Campus assembly room

Twombly library

converted to

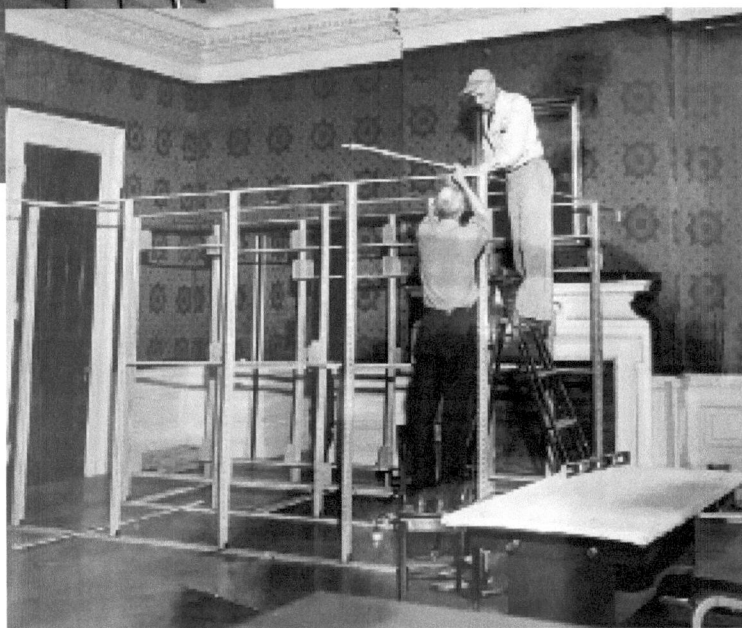

Temporary
campus library

Twombly
bedroom

converted to

Campus classroom

Converting the Former Carriage House to a Science Facility

The former carriage house was remodeled as a science building at the cost of over one and a quarter million dollars. When the first phase was completed in the fall semester, the building included five new laboratories and a nutrition and health laboratory.

Engineering and science facilities were constructed in the second of the three-phase science building conversion program and were ready for fall classes in 1959, including a new organic chemistry laboratory and nine classrooms.

Construction work continued on nutrition and health research laboratories and a nearly 200-seat science demonstration auditorium. By fall 1960, the third and final phase was completed, with six more laboratories for physics, chemistry, and biology.

Science Building laboratory stations

Carriage House
horse stalls

converted to

A functional science building

34

Refurbishing the Science Building roof

Science
Building
auditorium

Biology
laboratory

Athletic Facilities

A requiem for a bygone era was held on October 29, 1959 with an exhibition tennis match on the famous indoor clay tennis court of the former Twombly estate. The match marked the closing of the court in preparation for its remodeling into a gymnasium for the students. Students would soon play basketball in the new gym where once polite tennis was played. The court, part of the "Playhouse," was built in 1924 by Florence Vanderbilt Twombly for her daughter Ruth, a sports enthusiast. This was the setting in which Miss Twombly entertained the rich and famous of her day. The Playhouse contained the tennis court, heated swimming pool with showers and dressing room, wood-paneled salon, and a complete kitchen. The salon became the student lounge, with piano, TV, and hi-fi.

Unfortunately, when a new campus recreation center was constructed, the Playhouse was replaced by a classroom building. Despite consideration of converting it to classroom use, the project was abandoned when it was determined that such renovation would have a much higher cost than a new structure.

The Playhouse

Playhouse pool

Playhouse salon

Playhouse tennis court

converted to

Campus basketball court

Students swimming in the Playhouse pool

:

Utility Buildings Converted to an Arts Center

An oversized barn where workhorses were formerly housed became part of the University's Arts Center. The hayloft was converted into an art studio and the stable into modern classrooms for drama and offices for the faculty and literary publications. Sheep sheds were made into a performance hall, and storerooms for stage props. A shed was turned into an art gallery, lounge, and dormitory.

Florham barns

INITIAL GROUPS OF STUDENTS ON CAMPUS

Freshman
beanies

Women
students
relaxing

Registration
line

Food
line

Cotillion with fathers and daughters on December 13, 1959

Formal
dining

44

CAMPUS GROWTH

LLETIN

kinson University

r 3, 1959   EVERY TWO WEEKS

12,754 Students Flock to Classes

By HANS RATHJE

Enrollment at the university is still on the increase. The total number of students enrolled this year is 12,754. This figure constitutes a new record with an increase of 1,500 students over last year's enrollment. Teaneck is still in the lead with 6,517 students, followed by Rutherford with 4,633. Madison reports 1,604 students on this year's roster.

For the first time in the history of the university the I.B.M. robots of the new Statistical Office went into full swing, furnishing an early and accurate tabulation of enrollment.

The breakdown thus yields the following analysis:

At the Teaneck campus 2,005 students flock to the gates during the day, which is about 250 more than last year. Twice as many come at night, numbering 4,109, or about 490 more than in 1958.

At Rutherford 1,589 students attend day sessions compared with 1,625 last year. Although the drop is rather small with only 36 less, it's still a question of: how come? The evening school gained 12 here, making a total of 2,662 over 2,650 in 1958.

For its size, the Madison campus is catching up fast. There are 533 students enrolled here for the day sessions, topping last year's figure by 224. Their night school also nearly doubled its enrollment figure with 1,021, the 1958 count having been only 670.

The rest is made up of a miscellany category totaling 493 students in Teaneck, 582 in Rutherford and 50 in Madison. This last category includes 532 graduate students, 81 students who are registered at more than one campus, 43 high school students who have been admitted with superior records, and 186 dental students. There are 71 students enrolled in the Reading and Study Institute.

Photo Club Arranges December Beat Party

TEANECK — The Photography Club has succeeded in developing its program for the school year. Every Tuesday and Thursday ...

Italian Literature Topic of Review

Salvatore Quasimodo, winner of the 1959 Nobel Prize for Literature, and the "hermetic" school of poetry, which he helped to found, are discussed in the Fall number of The Literary Review, an international journal of contemporary writing published by Fairleigh Dickinson University.

The entire Fall number is devoted to recent Italian writing — poetry, short stories, essays on Italian fiction, literary criticism and the theatre.

Last spring The Review published a collection of modern Italian poems in English translation by Eric Sellin, including Quasimodo's short "hermetic" poem entitled "Oh Winter."

Other Italian poets discussed and translated in the Fall number include Carponi, Sereni, Libero, Luzi, Sinlsgalli, Gatto Penno Bertolucci, Pasolini, Spaziani, and Scottellaro. The translations are by the American poets Charles Guenther and Eric Sellin.

Among the authors of the thirteen Italian short stories included in The Review is Elsa Morante, wife of Moravia, and herself a distinguished writer of fiction. Other short stories are by Rea, Banti Manzini, Tobino, Cassola, Calvino Zolla, Landolfi, Flaiano, Buzzati Ortese and Bassani — all well-known in Italy and Europe generally but few of whom have as yet appeared in English translation.

Giacinto Spagnoletti — essayist, novelist and anthologist — discusses the major trends in recent Italian fiction. Claudio Gorlier, professor of American literature at the University of Turin, reviews Italian criticism. And Nicola Chiaramonte ...

Just one year after the campus opened in 1958, enrollment more than doubled. *The Bulletin*, then the student newspaper for the entire University, in its September 3, 1959 edition, reported that Madison had grown from 224 full-time day students to 533. Part-time evening numbers jumped from 670 to 1,021.

45

THE BULLETIN

MADISON CAMPUS EDITION

VOL. 2, NO. 1   MADISON, MORRIS CO., NEW JERSEY   SEPTEMBER 18, 1961

Student Enrollment Surges Upward Faculty Expands; Facilities Growing

950 Old and New Students Jam Campus As FDU Opens Fall Term in Heat Wave; New Teachers Bring Faculty up to 69

Under fair skies and a sizzling sun that sent thermometers into the high nineties, nearly a thousand undergraduates converged on Madison Campus of Fairleigh Dickinson University last week to score up the highest day enrollment in history.

The incoming freshman class numbered 311 — ten per cent above all previous freshman classes. Twenty-five names were added to the list of the university's teachers bringing the new total to 69.

As the torrid weather of the first three days of the week persisted, the matriculation process proceeded smoothly. First year students, despite the heat and the waiting in line, patiently went through the throes of registration, book-buying, arranging of class schedules and familiarizing themselves as much as possible with the unfrequented areas of the campus. When they had a moment to eat they solved the mysteries of the robot canteens.

Undergraduates who returned to assume their roles of upper classmen said they were excited at the influx of new students, larger by far than they had anticipated. Judy Wilson, president of the senior class, recalled her first days on the campus as a freshman four years ago:

All in all there were 276 of us and we had a choice of about three student extracurricular activities and everything was in the mansion then even the library. Now there are more than 60 out-of-class activities for the new student to choose from."

Veterans of the faculty spoke in retrospect of the educational facilities and their growth Mr. Malcolm Sturchio, head of the College of Science and Engineering pointed out that four years ago the college boasted of 3 teaching laboratories of which today there are 12. In 1958 the university had no research laboratories, now there are 8.

Dean Samuel Pratt expressed gratification at the growth of the Madison Campus, emphasizing the well-rounded facilities for a comprehensive undergraduate program.

"In the future," he told the freshmen, "efforts will be concentrated on deepening and enriching the academic life of students."

The dean called the attention of returning as well as new students to the university's expanded facility for the academic year 1961-62. He declared we have use of the outstanding undergraduate facilities in the country.

Two years later, September 1961, the campus had its own separate version of *The Bulletin* that told of 314 incoming freshmen and the addition of 25 faculty members, bringing the total to 69. The senior class president, Judy Wilson, noted that when she entered as a student she and her classmates had only three extracurricular activities available. Four years later, students had the choice of sixty. For the sciences, three teaching laboratories had become twelve, and eight research laboratories were made available when in 1958 there were none.

DESIGNING NEW CONSTRUCTION FOR LEARNING AND CREATIVITY: DEAN SAMUEL PRATT

Dr. Pratt, the first dean of the Florham-Madison campus, wrote these goals in 1963 on the occasion of announcing the plans for Twombly Hall, the campus' first residential dormitory. His ideas embody more than just a plan for a building, but encompass his broader educational philosphy as he developed the campus.

The Esthetic Goals

A basic educational goal of the University is that students understand, enjoy, and engage in some form of creativity in the arts while on campus and after graduation. While this goal is difficult to attain in the best of circumstances, the University has been fortunate in acquiring one of the world's most beautiful estates with outstanding buildings, gardens, and landscaping. Because of the superlative standards established by the Twombly family, the students are uniquely endowed environmentally. It is a priceless gift that the University must extend in its own architecture, both because of the need for art and because building design and the furnishing can either reinforce or contradict the teaching of esthetic. This is one of the reasons it was important to name the first new major building "Twombly Hall" for Mr. and Mrs. Hamilton McK Twombly.

Thus, in designing Twombly Hall, a hillside was selected that was organically related to the other buildings and which allowed a dramatic outline. The building was then oriented on the main axis of the Twombly family residence. While Georgian principles of architecture could not be used, the choice of white tile on exposed vertical columns was made for harmony with the limestone column of the Mansion. Landscaping, even to concrete walkways related to the older garden walks, has been designed on the same premise.

Architect's rendering of proposed residential complex

Furnishing choices were influenced again by the esthetic educational goal—examples are the simple functional lines of the desks in each room, the hanging of professional art in dining halls, lounges, and public areas, and the program of offering student art on loan for hanging in individual rooms.

The Scholarship Need

How to design a residential center so it reinforces scholarship aspirations is the question. This is accomplished, in part, by designing a variety of living quarters that offer changed living conditions to the students as they progress from freshman to graduate student with all the personal changes implied in the progression. In Twombly Hall, there are single and double rooms, suites, and graduate student and faculty apartments. The suites consist of two bedrooms, a living room, and bath with an adjacent private kitchen and dining room.

As an example of meeting special scholarship needs of upper-class students, it is expected that the suite floor will be reserved for a special senior group to be known as Junior Fellows. Financial assistance is now being sought for support of the Junior Fellows program. Each Fellow will be assigned to an academic department and will be required to assist academically by creating and directing special programs for students. The proposed Fellows program will be a significant innovation in many ways but the most important aspects are the enrichment of learning opportunities for the superior student, the bringing of students into academic leadership positions with the aim of broadening the non-class intellectual programs on the campus, and the symbolic value of rewarding students in a major way for high achievement, as the basic reason for attending college. The chances of success are significantly increased when the Fellows have common quarters. Further, the presence of the Junior Fellows in so prominent a position in the living center will stand also as a constant stimulus to lower classmen to strive for academic distinction.

The Need for Student–Faculty Contact

Another aspect of the educational outlook of the University is the great importance given to close personal interaction among students and faculty: Twombly Hall reflects this in a number of ways. There are faculty apartments, for younger faculty without children, which are centers of informal discussion. Many faculty feel it is a pleasure as well as an obligation to dine occasionally with students. The residential student government is increasingly creating both formal and informal contact through student-faculty debates, faculty-led discussions, teas, and faculty-student weekends in New York City.

The Need for Individuality

When visitors tour the dining rooms of Twombly, they will discover not one dining room, but four, each furnished differently. The presently occupied sections have two dining rooms, one furnished in modernistic metal and plastic in a room with light colors, and the second furnished in handcrafted pine from Maine set in an appropriate decor. One of the two additional dining rooms now being built will be furnished in formal

English dining style, while the other will be in old American tavern style.

The educational reasoning is in part esthetic and, in part, an attitude about students. Just as students differ in such matters as curricular interests and leisure time pursuits, they differ in emotions and attitudes about dining manners, dress, and appreciation of furnishings and art. Individuality in these matters should be encouraged. By offering attractive alternatives in dining, one more contribution is made to the general objective of helping each student seek his or her own pattern in life. In the curricular and co-curricular program, similar efforts are made to give the individual realistic choices. For instance, in the selection of courses, two specific devices used are honors programs and selected studies. Both of these direct the student to work on problems uniquely interesting to him to help shape his own learning pattern. Extending choice to dining and other areas of life on the campus rounds out the opportunities and gives the student a greater sense of person.

Thc Need for Broad Interaction

The need for privacy of the person must be balanced with the need to assure broad social interaction. From a group of applicants four or five times larger than can be accommodated, the freshman class each year is carefully selected with an emphasis on individuality and uniqueness. The educational purposes of this diversity could be defeated if the residential hall design exerted through spatial relations a constriction rather than expansion of interpersonal exchange. Thus, in Twombly Hall, the two sleeping and study masses have been related to a large commons. At the same time, smaller areas are provided in each sleep area which favor the organization of smaller student groupings. The overall design encourages formation of a complex student grouping pattern. The whole is tied together by a formal student residence government body that devises and supervises the code of living in all residences and which also relates the residence student to the non-dormitory student.

The Need for Campus and Society Contact

On a campus designed equally for residential and commuting students, care must be taken that segregation does not occur. In part, this involves the design of a lounge where the dormitory students are expected to provide programs for the non-residential student and, in part, involves the design of the total campus. In the next residence development phase, service facilities needed by all students will be constructed so as to create a flow of all students to the residential area. This is considered important because of the conception that a college student should not divorce himself from the broader society but rather should be asserting himself in it. Individual responsibilility and initiative can hardly be developed in an atmosphere that isolates the student from society and favors an attitude that responsibility is for tomorrow—after the magical moment of receiving a diploma. For this reason, our educational programs include service by students in community centers of the area, field trips, and study projects in economically and culturally submerged areas in the United States, humanitarian projects such as fund-raising for leukemia research, student-led symposia on great social issues, and foreign study centers and travel programs.

The interaction of dormitory and commuting students is vital educationally. The commuting student brings to a campus a fresh breath of the world "outside." The dormitory student is the core of the campus community. Together, the students form a comprehensive learning environment organically related to issues beyond the person and beyond the campus.

Samuel Pratt,
Campus Dean, 1963

Twombly Hall
construction

Twombly Hall
Lounge
Construction

Twombly Hall
dorm room

53

Orangerie Developed into Campus Library

The architectural rendering of the first phase of the million-dollar library was prepared in July 1959 to convert what was once an orangerie into a modern library building. Then called the Friendship Library, it opened in January 1961 with study carrels for 300 students and 60,000 volumes.

As the result of grants and gifts, a major expansion was undertaken in 1965 to provide space for 200,000 additional volumes on four levels. For this project, the University received a $261,653 grant from the Higher Education Facilities Act and another $200,000 from corporations and individuals.

Architect's plan for the library

Library under construction

EVENTS OF A WEEK

This calendar of events, called Faculty Bulletin, is the very first schedule issued during the initial semester of the campus.

FACULTY BULLETIN
Fairleigh Dickinson University

FLORHAM - MADISON CAMPUS

VOLUME I	No. I	October 10, 1958

Saturday	October 11th	8:30 P.M.	Dixie Land Jazz Concert - Great Hall Mrs. D'Asaro and Mr. Sturchio, Faculty representatives
Monday	October 13th	4:00 P.M.	Swimming (Women) Life Guard - Iris Bauer
		4:00 P.M.	University Choir Mr. Mitcheltree - Faculty Advisor
		5:00 P.M.	Ping - Pong Club - Playhouse Lounge Mr. Riggs, Faculty Advisor
Tuesday	October 14th	9:00 A.M. to 12:00 M.	Student Elections
		10:00 A.M.	Convocation - Great Hall The Honorable Peter H. B. Frelinghuysen, Republican candidate for Congress from this district
		11:00 A.M.	Dr. Peter Sammartino, President of the University
		2:15 P.M.	Figure Control Club - Playhouse Mrs. D'Asaro - Faculty Advisor
		3:15 P.M.	Swimming (Women) Life Guard - Kathryn Allen
		3:30 P.M.	Meeting of the Women Dormitory Students to plan weekend activities - Sock-Hop Room 9
		4:00 P.M.	Visit by Dr. Arthur Stoll, Chairman of the Board of Directors of Sandoz, Inc
		4:00 P.M.	Toboganing Club - Room 20 Dr. Lois Pratt - Faculty Advisor
Wednesday	October 15th	9:30 A.M.	FDU Racquets Club - Room 9 Mr. Meyer - Faculty Advisor
		10:00 A.M.	Visits by High School Students - Senior Class
		2:00 P.M.	Swimming (women) Life Guard - Kathryn Allen
		4:00 - 6:00 P.M.	Synchronized Swimming Mrs. F. J. Ryan, Instructress
		4:00 P.M.	Hiking Club - Room 20 Professor Rice - Faculty Advisor

6247-1-8

VOLUME I		No. 1	October 10, 1958

2

Thursday	October 16th	9:00 A.M. - 3:00 P.M.	Administrative Clinic of the New Jersey Secondary School Principals Association
		4:00 P.M.	Swimming (Men) Life Guard - Horton Land
		3:00 P.M.	Bowling Club Meeting Morris and Essex Lanes, Columbia Bridge Road, Florham Park
		5:00 P.M.	Gourmet Club - Room 9 Dr. and Mrs. Pratt - Faculty Advisors
Friday	October 17th	4:00 P.M.	Swimming (Men) Life Guard - Douglas Messineo
Saturday	October 18th	10:00 A.M.	Synchronized Swimming Mrs. F. J. Ryan, Instructress
		2:00 - 4:00 P.M.	Swimming (Co-Ed) Life Guard - Horton Land
		3:00 P.M. - 5:00 P.M.	Allegro Club Tour

Students should understand that course substitutions in any curriculum can be approved only by advisors. Advisors are listed below:

Engineering, Physics	Dr. Taylor
Chemistry	Mr. Sturchio
English and Liberal Arts	Mr. Savage
Biology	Mr. Muschio
Psychology	Dr. Alven
History	Mr. Riggs
Economics, Sociology	Dr. Lois Prat
Mathematics	Mrs. Gilbert
Medical Arts	Mr. Sturchio
School of Business	
1. Accounting	Mr. Feldman
2. All other	Mr. Rice
Education	Dr. Irwin
Graduate School	Dr. Samuel Pr

DOROTHEA CREAMER MEMORIES

Dorothea Creamer, the original circulation librarian on the Florham Campus, wrote the following letter to Dr. Peter Sammartino in 1977 at his request when she retired after twenty years of service. She shares many unique memories of the campus' origin and her relationships with students. For two decades, Mrs. Creamer—as everyone called her—was a respected and well-loved member of the campus community.

In this remembrance, she neglects to mention the supply of ties and jackets required for male students using the library from 1958 to 1965.

Dr. Sammartino,

You have asked for my memories of my first years at our Madison Campus. There are so many starting with Dr. George Nelson, the director of the University Libraries. I had been working at the Boonton Holmes Library on a part-time basis. I had started back in 1930 working at Newark Public Library when Miss Beatrice Wonsor was the director. One of the regular users of the Holmes Library was attending Rutherford Campus of FDU. She suggested I go to the Madison Twombly estate and apply for a position as a library was to be established. I stated that I had no University Library experience and decided not to apply. Two days later, I received a telephone call from a Dr. George Nelson asking me to please meet him at Madison two days later, approximately May 25[th,] 1958. I shall never forget my visit at the Mansion and my long talk with Dr. Nelson. I also met one of my dearest friends, Sarah Sullivan, who had worked for the Twombly estate prior to working for FDU. I must tell you that I was in the Mansion when I was 13. My grandfather, Mr. Ernest Hothorn, owned a large summer home in Succasunna, N.J. My grandfather had a lot of horses as all the grandchildren over 8 had to ride every day. He purchased some of the horses owned by

the Twomblys. My grandfather's home is now "Clyde's Restaurant" on Route 10.

After a long two-hour talk with Dr. Nelson, I agreed to start working June 4, 1958. The library was to be established in the Formal Dining Room (Book Stack Area); the former Twombly library with the black marble fireplace was to be a library study room. The formal living room behind the huge Great Hall fireplace was to be the Reference Room, with wooden book shelves. A desk was placed near the door so that a librarian could check books in and out and help students who needed guidance with reference material. The steam room next to the formal dining room was used as a work area where books were recorded and prepared for circulation. All work was done on tables, as there were no desks in the first months at Madison. My first desk was a discarded desk from Allied Chemical Corporation, which has done much for the Madison Campus.

My first meeting with Dr. & Mrs. Sammartino was in June 1958 when they came to the campus for a literary seminar. At that time I met Dr. Heinz and Dagmar MacKinson, a very special and loyal couple who have done much to help Fairleigh Dickinson University grow.

The first summer flew by and September 1958 arrived with the first group of students. Some were dorm students and many were commuting students.

During the summer, the staff who were working were treated weekly to the music which a Mr. Higgins would play on the great organ, which was located in the Great Hall next to the ballroom. Many of us would call out play this, play that! It was hard to work as the sound was so beautiful. I have long been a lover of organ music.

I should mention the bathroom problem when the septic tanks in the back of the Mansion were replaced with larger ones. We parked our cars in front of the mansion and those of us who had large cars would take turns driving a carful to the Athletic Building so that we could use the bathroom facilities next to the large swimming pool. This went on for about three weeks. We were a friendly group and all worked together to help start our Madison campus.

The arrival of our first live-on-campus students was quite an event. The young ladies were housed on the top floor of the mansion. More of the young ladies were housed on the second floor over the now Hartman Lounge and Sarah Sullivan Lounge. I remember so vividly coming to work one morning, parking my car and I looked up at the front of the mansion, something I have never tired of doing. The architecture is so beautiful, the magnificence of the building, is breathtaking. Thanks to Dr. Sammartino, the building will remain!

One of the young ladies had turned 20 and had had a party. The empty beer cans were

58

stacked in the shape of a pyramid! I and other staff were amused as young people were starting back in 1958 to defy rules and regulations! I am afraid Dr. Pratt was not amused; he is a brilliant man but unfortunately had little understanding of young people. Granted, I did not approve of many things young people did then and do now, but times have changed for the majority. If you want to gain the trust of young people one must listen!

I remember so well the first debutante ball that was held in the great ballroom. Some of the staff worked with the young ladies so that they would walk down the grand staircase with their long skirts, which had hoops under them. They were taught to keep their balance when bowing.

In the spring of 1958-59 the housemother fell and broke her leg. Dr. Pratt, the Campus Dean, sent for me and asked if I would take over till the semester ended. I agreed and brought my clothes and settled down in the huge room at the top of the main stairway. Each day I would climb the 56 stairs and become housemother. I had raised four daughters, so I was prepared for much that I would see. The mess that many of the large rooms had become with five and six girls living together was amazing. I would check the rooms each evening and quietly say the room looked like a dump. Later I would be asked to come back and see the rooms that would have been cleaned up. I spent most evenings with ten or twelve young ladies studying, and then had a long conversation about their homes, families, and what they hoped to accomplish after college. Some evenings we would send out for sandwiches and a very warm happy evening it would be. I still keep in touch with a few of our first students; to this day I have a long list of alumni who keep in touch, they let me know when a baby arrives and I started many years ago making a pair of booties. I still do and have made over 60 pairs in the past ten years. I am so proud of so many of our Madison graduates.

I remember the morning I drove on campus in 1960 and saw a few students looking up at the water towers, which are opposite the Athletic building. The three water towers had been marked by one of our energetic male students who had climbed the ladder and painted SCOTCH on one side, RYE and RUM on the other two. This was during the time when drinking legally was still 21! I must remind you that there were no Coke machines, young men used to wear jackets and ties to classes and when using the library. Young ladies were not permitted to wear slacks or shorts anywhere near campus.

I remember one morning in 1959 coming down the back stairway and found three tea-spoons on the floor by the big steel door on the ground floor. I knew instantly as I picked up the three teaspoons, how the young ladies had been returning after hours. I walked down the main hall to Dr. Pratt's office. I knocked on his door and was told to come in. I walked into his office and laid the three spoons on his desk and stated this is how the young ladies are returning late at night and getting into the dorms. I had to show Dr. Pratt how one puts the bowl of the spoon over the catch on the door! The door was closed when the guard would go by and check; when a young lady would return late and get by the guard without being seen, the door would open! The spoon would drop to the floor and the <u>late</u> student would dash to the third floor and forget to pick up the spoon. The procedure had been going on in colleges for years.

In the early years convocations were held and when possible administration and faculty would attend. Convocations were discontinued in the late 60s as students rebelled, to their loss I would say. I often wondered why some of the rebels came to college with their filthy long hair, matted beards, dirty jeans, looking like unmade beds! They rebelled against so many things that most of us had accepted all our lives and now many of the radicals have accepted!

There were also the students who wanted an education and were willing to work for it. I chaperoned many parties, dances, and lectures in the early days.

The early graduation exercises were so special—all three campuses joined and came to Madison as no one disputes the fact that the Florham Madison Campus is beautiful. The cars all over, traffic tie ups—lack of bathroom facilities were all accepted. All at Madison would pray for days that the weather would be fair. The bagpipe band playing, the trustees, President and faculty with the graduates in caps and gowns was a very impressive sight. I have attended twenty graduation exercises and will continue to do so!

I remember the wonderful party that was held in the Great Hall and ballroom honoring Dr. Sammartino, who has done so much to keep Fairleigh Dickinson University the special school that it has become. The great hall and ballroom were filled with many friends, faculty and staff who had admired Dr. Sammartino as a fine man and for all he had and still does accomplish, not without his wife, Sally Sammartino. A scholarship has been established in Dr. Sammartino's name. A buffet supper was served and enjoyed by all.

I remember the dinner honoring Prof. Louis Rice of the business college for having taught fifty years. The dinner was held in the great ballroom and was attended by many friends and former faculty from other schools who had worked with Prof. Rice. We were also treated to the music of the great organ played by Mr. Edward Broadhead, the campus Librarian, who had an additional masters in Music as well as in Library Science.

The annual faculty party every September was held in the Athletic Building in the Louis Rice lounge or, if the weather permitted, on the great veranda overlooking the Grecian gardens and fountain. An informal gathering making it possible for faculty, old, new and administration personnel to become acquainted. In the early days, 59-60-61—all were invited to a dinner held at Rutherford, making it possible for all three campus faculty, wives, and administrative personnel to get to know each other. As the University grew, the dinners became cocktail parties held at each campus on a rotating basis every third year. The University finally ended this in the early 70s as the financial crunch forced many cutbacks, such as the awards ceremony—5-10-15-20 years at F.D.U. I was one of the few who felt that each faculty and administrative staff could contribute five dollars apiece and once again the Faculty party in the fall could be continued. Madison Campus holds an annual awards picnic in June as it is no longer possible to have all three campuses meet together.

I remember the day the gold tapestry was removed from the great hall. The days that it took for the men to carefully remove the chandelier that hung in the center of the great ballroom, the crystals would not stand the noise that large crowds would create. This beautiful chandelier now hangs in Macculloch Hall in Morristown, a beautiful historic home in Morristown, New Jersey.

The dedication of the library, which was built on to the Orangerie where Mrs. Twombly kept her huge potted plants and trees for display. As part of the library, it became a study room.

The huge affair honouring the Duke and Duchess of York from England. A huge tent was set up for the dinner. Cocktail parties were held in the great ballroom, on the veranda, and the Orangerie of the library. The weather was beautiful and I am glad that I was able to be in the library and see part of the festivities. I also remember: the huge snow storms, which brought all traffic on the campus roads to a standstill as there are three miles of roads at Florham Madison campus.

The day the air conditioner unit on the roof of the library broke. The windows in the library do not open. The weather was in the 90s and we somehow managed to exist for two weeks.

The night that I had stayed late as one of the desk circulation employees was unable to come to work. At about 9:30, the evening custodian asked if I could come downstairs to the new addition where thousands of back periodicals were piled on the floor awaiting the installation of steel shelving. It had rained for two days. I went down to the basement and found water pouring into the basement. I had to have help so I climbed the stairs and called the dorms and asked for Stuart Kipilman, one of my super excellent student workers. I told him what was happening and that I needed help. In no time 20 young men and women came running to the basement and thousands of periodicals were saved because of their help. I wanted to treat them to sandwiches and soda afterwards; they all said no. I still keep in touch with some of these alumni.

I remember our lunches in the faculty dining room in the mansion basement talking with Willie Ley, the great scientist, and Dr. Alveen, the psychologist. Those were days of wonderful conversations, get togethers that anyone who was there does not forget!

The parties that were held in the gym for various fund raising benefits. The concert that the "Up With People" singers held, the huge open air concerts that were held on the library lawn with hundreds of towns people attending.

At one time in the 60s, the Athletic banquets were held off campus. Then the Athletic awards were held in the gym. The department has grown tremendously in the last ten years.

The science department, which was very small in the early years, has grown and many of our graduates have become doctors and dentists and researchers.

I could go on for pages but it is not possible to do that and still get this to you, Dr. Sammartino.

In closing, I will tell you that on Sat., July 15, 78, I went to 15 Knollwood Dr., Hanover, the home of Raymond Kwong, a Masters graduate at Madison, and his wife, Lilly Lee Kwong, Madison ((1964), a teacher with many years of teaching in the Frelinghuysen School. They have a beautiful 10-month-old daughter named Lisette. Ray's sister, Casey Kwong Birmingham (1971), and her husband, Tom Birmingham (1972), were there. What a wonderful evening babbling about their days at Madison. Lilly had been one of my early student workers in the library. Her husband, Ray, cooked the Chinese dinner, which was super. We talked for hours about the different alumni that each of us has kept in touch with. It makes me feel so good when I can see some of alumni "children."

The friends I have made during my 19 years at Madison I treasure and I loved being a part of Madison and watching it grow. I always get a magical feeling when I drive down the main road towards the Mansion in the early evening and see the lights on. One has to see it to realize the magnificence of the architecture!

I hope you can read my writing. I do not have a typewriter at my disposal.

Thank you for asking me for my memories of Madison.

I trust you are both well.

As Ever
Dorothea Creamer
Madison – 58-77

P.S. I was honoured by many friends and faculty and alumni at dinner at Rod's that 175 attended. I have a huge album of pictures to treasure as I do not enjoy retirement. I keep hoping I'll find a part- time position; however, I do keep in touch with Sarah [Sullivan] and other close friends who also hold special memories of Madison FDU.

MEMORIES OF THREE RESIDENTIAL STUDENTS

Clara Warcola Bondinell, Lilly Lee Kwong, and Pat Moran were residential students during the first years of the Florham Campus, Pat arriving in 1959, Lilly in 1960, and Clara in 1961. They were friends then, and their friendship has continued through the years. They shared memories and photographs of their experiences as pioneers at a growing institution in the midst of defining its mission and developing its facilities, and were present when the first dormitory, Twombly Hall, was opened and when the library was built. They witnessed the construction taking place and the campus growing in student numbers and academic opportunities.

Pat, Clara, and Lilly in 2018

As first-generation students, they came with no preconceptions about what lay ahead for them in college. They knew they were participating in a new creation, a situation that they found offered many advantages. Key to the experience was the wealth of opportunities and the openness of administrators to new ideas for clubs and activities. They created and participated in a range of roles and organizations. Clara says, "Opportunities were here; you only had to take advantage of them!" Looking back today, they consider their education and life at Florham a very positive experience.

Because the new campus had so many roles to fill, they were given positions of responsibility, compensated by the university rather than a work-study budget. During her sophomore through senior years, Lilly served as weekend switchboard operator at a time when calls to the main number were distributed manually. Clara, who was editor of the newly created student newspaper, *The Metro*, worked in the public relations office. In addition, she served as student editor of Lois Pratt's journal, *University Woman*. Pat worked in the library. All three babysat for Pamela Pratt, the toddler daughter of Campus Dean Samuel Pratt and sociology professor Lois Pratt, and were paid by the Pratts.

Clara majored in secondary education, with a concentration in history; Lilly in elementary education; and Pat in business with an accounting specialty.

Choosing the Florham Campus

Pat's journey from an isolated farm in rural Ireland was certainly the most unusual. She explains the unique circumstances of her admission:

"My relatives applied to Rutgers, Seton Hall & FDU, Madison. FDU accepted me, and I assume it was because they needed students as my diploma from Ireland was a beautiful scroll, edged in Celtic designs similar to the ones in The Book of Kells and completely in Gaelic. A letter of recommendation from the nuns was of little help as they had never been asked to recommend a student for higher education. Acceptance to university in Ireland at that time was entirely based on grades."

Not only was her application singular, so was the transformation of her circumstances with the radical shift from farm to estate:

"I had very little knowledge of the history of the campus when I started. I arrived in the US on August 29 and school started about a week or so later. I assumed that all universities in the US were beautiful castles on magnificent estates like Florham. Living in the mansion was like I died and went to heaven. I had just left the farm in Ireland where I was born and where meals required growing the vegetables, milking cows, making butter and bread, and now I could just pick up whatever I wanted from the cafeteria and push the dirty dishes into a hole in the wall and walk away. I had been orphaned and as the oldest sibling it was my responsibility to be the homemaker. My experience was so different from that of my American classmates."

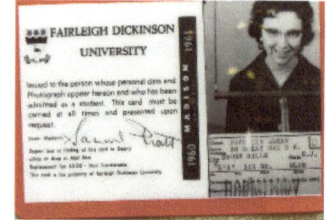

Pat must have adjusted to America quickly because, with her business/accounting degree, she went on to attain an MBA at FDU's Teaneck Campus, the only woman in her classes for her four years of part-time enrollment, though several other women had graduated before her. After graduating, she discovered her choice presented her with serious challenges, however, in the work world. She was faced with contempt at "the very idea of an auditor being a woman!"

While a visit home by Pat would have involved a plane ride and probably various journeys from airport to farm, Lilly was only a short train trip away from her home in Manhattan, a basic reason for choosing the campus. She explains:

"I went there because it was in close proximity to New York City and accessible transportation. I had to work on the weekends in the City, which I did my freshman year. I would walk to Convent Station to take the train into Hoboken and then take the PATH into the City. Often I hitched a ride with a fellow classmate who was going out to Long Island or into the City, get dropped off near a subway station and then travel home."

Clara had grown up in Manville, New Jersey, and also found the campus convenient. Her younger sister followed her to Florham as a student in the mid-1960s.

Lilly (left) and friends on campus

Living in the Mansion

For the first few years of the campus, women students lived in rooms on the second and third floors and west wing of the Mansion. The men lived in the wings around the courtyard and in a group of structures called the Quad, then located in the present area of the Monninger Center, the Student Center, and the Chaîne building.

Lilly tells of being one of the few students on campus to own a car, a 1957 Chrysler that she used to get to student teaching. It was parked by the Quad and took almost an hour to warm up with much engine rattling, with the men complaining about the noise that woke them up.

The Mansion, in addition to its residential function, served academic and administrative purposes on the first floor. Pat notes that in her initial years she never had to leave the Mansion for residence, classes, or food. The Science Building also provided classrooms.

Lilly remembers:

"I had two other roommates and we lived in one of the large rooms in the mansion facing the long drive towards the building. During the first year there, some of the rooms were still intact. The rooms on the first floor housed the library—which still had the original tapestries on the walls and were later auctioned off—the bursar's office, admissions office, dean of student affairs office and the "ballroom" in which small group convocations were held. Most memorable was the organ, which was played on Sunday mornings. The music could be heard throughout the mansion since there were pipes throughout the building. The cafeteria and bookstore were housed in the lower floor of the building."

Pat in her dorm room

Twombly Hall Dormitory

When the first dormitory, Twombly Hall, opened in the fall of 1961, students were living in the Mansion, temporarily crowded into what became classrooms. Clara remembers that when the dorm opened on a rainy day, they had to pack quickly and carry their suitcases to the new building, sliding down a muddy slope because steps hadn't yet been built.

Twombly Hall was organized with men assigned to the first and fourth floors, women on floors 2, 3, 5 and 6. It had four dining rooms with a different dress code for each dining room. Students had to dress for dinner as they did for classes and study in the library, men in ties and jackets and women in skirts.

A Sense of Florham's History

Although the three women were impressed by the buildings and grounds, they were not informed of the history of Florham. Clara suggests that Dean Pratt and others were so focused on the complexities of creating a campus, planning for the future, that they didn't have time to consider the past.

Clara in yearbook

In effect, they took their Gilded Age surroundings for granted, appreciating details without awareness of their origins. For example, they enjoyed the organ concerts, but students were not allowed to play the instrument. They were impressed by the frescos on the walls of the Playhouse pool [created by Robert Winthrop Chanler]. The large rock on the drive to the Mansion—later named Reuter's Rock after German professor Walter Reuter—was "sacred." Students were forbidden to tamper with it, certainly not paint announcements on it as they do today. Students did sit in the Italian Garden to study.

Activities Beyond the Classroom

The alums remembered that "you made your own entertainment, playing bridge or ...." There was a theater group; card parties; a B. Altman Fashion show; dances (a luau, once)—"you could look out from Mansion windows and see dancing below"; lacrosse, basketball, tennis, and other sports.

Pat Moran notes that there was a bowling alley and a roller skating rink in Florham Park. Commuting classmates with cars would pick up residential students and take them places. She remembers, "a bunch of them taking me to see the wonders New Jersey had to offer, things I would not have experienced on the farm back in Ireland. I remember one of those adventures to an amusement park. I asked them not to put me on any fast or crazy ride and as we drove up I saw a ride coming in slowly and told them that was for me. It was the roller coaster coming to a stop. You can imagine their delight on seeing me ride that thing. I have never been on one since, but they remained my friends."

Because of the curfew for women that forbade them to leave the Mansion at night, they occasionally pooled their money and had one of the men buy and send pizza up on the dumbwaiter from the basement.

Remembered Faculty and Staff

Although the women found limited interaction with faculty outside the classroom, certain individual professors made a strong impression. The faculty and staff they singled out were Nish Najarian of student activites, Robert Markoff of history, Warren Ward of biology, Winberg Chai of political science (later author of *The Girl from Purple Mountain* and other books), Saul Feldman of business, and John Fritz of history for his equestrian connection. Dr. Chai invited a small group to his home for Chinese New Year dinner. They recall Lois Pratt riding her bicycle around campus from the Dean's residence in the Gatehouse.

Lilly singles out "Dr. Stephen Goode in the English Department, Dr. Chai in the History Department, Dr. Ward and Dr. Griffo in the Science Department, Dr. Louis Gordon in the Music Department, and Dr. Albert Hartman in the Education Department."

Other Students

As young residential undergraduates, the women felt themselves very different from the veterans and other older students.

Lilly considered herself the only non-white student on campus, but there was also a contingent of foreign students from Africa, mainly Kenya, and Indonesia on campus.

Students had little contact with the Teaneck and Rutherford campuses and no sense of any differences in curriculum or reciprocal programs. They considered themselves country cousins forgotten by the other two campuses.

Protests

The women recall the time other students, mainly male, hung the Dean in effigy to demand Coke machines in the dorm. Because university President Peter Sammartino was a health food fanatic, the vending machines offered only healthy products.

Memories of a Commuter Student

Richard (Dick) Wellbrock, BA 1960, MBA 1964, has shared his memories as an advanced-standing commuter student during the initial years of the campus, as well as his ongoing relationship with Fairleigh Dickinson University.

Dick is a Certified Management Consultant and the President of Wellbrock, Inc., a firm engaged to provide consulting services in small business management, new business start-up activity, public and private offerings, organizational development, mergers and acquisitions, real estate syndication, contract employment, and employee leasing. His background also includes a long history of serving in the position of chairman, with companies engaged in photograph and film processing and community banking. His Ph.D. is from Walden University in philosophy, with a specialty in education. He has served as Vice-Chairman of Raritan Valley Community/College.

**Dick Wellbrock
as a student**

I was the first and sole graduate of the Madison campus in February 1960. In June of 1960 one more baccalaureate degree was granted as were two associate degrees. My degree is in Economics.

I decided to attend this campus because I had taken a number of courses on the campus during the summer prior to FDU welcoming its first four-year class of about 100 students in the fall of 1958. I concluded that the campus was close to my home in Summit, and I realized that the class size would be small.

As an undergraduate on the Madison campus, you belonged to one of the two communities that would have been found on that campus. Most of the students were day hops,

**Dick Welbrock
today**

71

and for them there was little desire or need for extracurricular activities. With the admission of the first four-year freshman program, dorms were created on the upper floors of the mansion. For the dorm students, almost immediately upon arriving on campus a need for a sense of involvement emerged. Slowly, clubs and other activities surfaced even in the fall of the first year of dorm students. Among the first activities developed in that initial fall awakening was a touch football league.

My class level was deemed "advanced standing." As a result, I had to take classes in Rutherford and Teaneck in addition to Madison. Much of the advanced standing class transferred from other educational institutions or from one of the other FDU campuses. Many of the male students were veterans of the Korean War and were enrolled at this time because the GI Education Bill was about to expire for those who did not start their college effort by the bill's concluding date.

The advanced standing group approximated forty students. Most of the veteran students had working wives. For the 1950s, working wives was not the norm, particularly if the wives were mothers. The veterans had very little interest in any extracurricular activity.

In spite of a resident student population, the majority of the students lived at home. I can recall no friend who was a dorm student, and that might be because my friends were advanced standing and many of them had jobs and/or spouses.

What is noteworthy with this group was the small size of the advanced student classes. My sociology class was typical of the class size for this level of student. That class had six students and we met in the entering gate carriage house where the dean of the campus and his wife lived.

Their names were Dean Samuel Pratt and his wife, Dr. Lois Pratt. Dr. Pratt served coffee during her sociology class session. It was a great class because being small in size, all were attentive. It was obvious who was or was not prepared.

Bear in mind that the student day population was not large in contrast with the number of students attending night school. In fact, the number of day students was dwarfed by the population of night attendees where the number of students in a class was considerably larger than the size of a class for day students. Noteworthy was the total lack of any interest in campus life of the night student. FDU for the night student was, then and probably is still, related to the distance a student must travel after a day of work.

My children, with two baccalaureate degrees and one masters' from the Florham campus, had different approaches to their "college days." The two baccalaureate degree holders lived on campus. Each found activities in which to be engaged. The daughter who earned an MBA lived at home but earned free tuition by working as an intern in the Rothman School of Entrepreneurial Studies. In some ways, her tenure was more meaningful than that of her brother and sister because she met interesting people and was involved in many types of initiatives and outreach programs.

I enjoyed my undergraduate days in Madison and when asked to attend a graduate fund-raising group, decided to attend. Subsequently, I joined the group, agreed to write letters to graduates and call graduates to seek contributions. I found the connection to be interesting and stimulating. I would guess that my first gift was about $10 and was made about three years after I graduated with a BA and before I earned the MBA in 1964. We have been donors for fifty years.

Every year for many years I agreed to write letters and to make phone calls on behalf of FDU. When Frank Mertz, who was well known to me, became President, he was aware that the Wellbrocks had been meaningful donors and requested that I join the President's Advisory Committee as a small business. There were four meetings a year, at which the emphasis was always on the financial condition of the institution, and the outreach of the members of this committee to other corporations or foundations which had the capacity to support FDU. I was flattered to be a member of such a committee, which was composed of the senior-most officers of very major companies, particularly pharmaceutical companies. I do think I held my own as to personal financial contributions and to the analysis and discussion of the presented issues.

When Frank Mertz retired, President Adams did not maintain the President's Advisory Committee. I was introduced to a very newly arrived President [J. Michael] Adams. He took a very incisive interest in my role as Vice-Chairman of Raritan Valley Community College. Consequently, we collaborated in establishing a prototypical approach to FDU expansion by creating a number of degree opportunities on the campus of Raritan Valley Community College and ultimately other community college campuses. In part this type of venture nullified the need to create campus satellites elsewhere. I believe the community college campus model continues to be an important FDU initiative.

The contribution of Peter Sammartino to offer education opportunity in the form of a junior college or a dental school was not recognized by the general population or that he was a man of vision and leadership. Ultimately, his two-year education philosophy was recognized as needed by the State of New Jersey when it established a community college system which proved Sammartino's thesis that an individual need not earn a baccalaureate degree to improve that person's future economic achievement. The State of New Jersey filched another Sammartino innovation, and that was to create a medical school which confirmed that Sammartino was correct in creating a dental school to respond to the state dental need. The dental school was absorbed by the NJ College of Medicine and Denistry.

Remembering My Years at Florham: Dr. R. Gordon Perry

R. Gordon Perry entered the Madison Campus as a student in 1960, received BA degrees in business administration and biology and went on to earn a PhD in biology at Rutgers University. He then returned to the campus as a faculty member and by the time he retired had served as chair of the Department of Biological & Allied Health Sciences.

During the summer before my senior year in high school, my father had taken me to several colleges in New Jersey, Pennsylvania, and Maryland as possible places to attend after high school graduation. I was really not interested in living away from home and was more interested in attending a school where I could commute from home and, at the same time, continue with my part-time job at a camera shop in Caldwell. Although I had not considered Fairleigh Dickinson University at that time, our family doctor recommended that I visit the new campus that FDU was opening on the former Florham Estate in Florham Park. Upon his recommendation, I decided to visit the new campus in the spring of 1959 and to pick up an application for admission.

This was my first drive to the Florham Park area and I was impressed with the pleasant drive out of Florham Park, down the two-lane road through the swampland on Columbia Turnpike, and past a small Morristown Municipal Airport. It appeared so far away! As I made my way to Madison Avenue, I passed several mansions, the College of Saint Elizabeth, and then the long red brick wall surrounding Florham. As I entered Florham through a beautiful set of large black iron gates, I drove on a white gravel road past the gatehouse which served as the residence of the Campus Dean, Dr. Samuel

Pratt and his wife, Dr. Lois Pratt, who taught classes in sociology. I then drove through a wooded area leading to a tunnel under the Lackawanna Railroad tracks. After passing through the tunnel, I drove to a crossroad and continued ahead on the white gravel road leading to the mansion. I remember my first view of the mansion and its surroundings and thought that the entire place was absolutely beautiful! I remember a number of unique plantings and was surprised that the lawn areas were so well kept, especially considering that the estate had been unoccupied for some time.

As I continued forward, the mansion was separated from the lawn area by a beautiful

wall covered with evergreen Euonymous and large posts on either side of the drive. A building, I later learned was the Orangerie, and part of a large greenhouse complex, was located on the right side of the drive. It was unoccupied, overgrown with vines and other vegetation, and appeared to have a number of glass panels broken. The original horse stable, later used to house the fleet of Rolls Royces, was located a distance to the left side of the mansion and was in the process of being converted into the future Science Building. Also on the left side was the original Playhouse, complete with indoor pool and tennis courts, which was unoccupied and undergoing renovation.

The mansion was partially covered with ivy and had black shutters. I entered the house through the massive main door constructed of mahogany. It opened effortlessly, considering its size. On either side of the main entrance, there were additional entrances with smaller mahogany doors that all led into the main hall. Since the main part of Florham, the 180 acres containing the mansion and related buildings, had been purchased by the University in 1957, and the first class entered in 1958, the enrollment was small and educational facilities were at a minimum.

Upon entering the great hall, a small room containing a switchboard was located on the left side, and the Office of the Dean was located beyond it in what was originally the Twombly library. Straight ahead, behind the main fireplace, was the original dining room, now the location of the campus library with its walls covered in dark red silk fabric. On the right side of the great hall, a large console and some pipes for the Aeolian-Skinner pipe organ were located. Most pipes, including some very large ones, were located out of sight in the back. The right end of the hall opened into the original drawing room, which was used by the University for convocations and assemblies. At the opposite end of the Great Hall, a pantry was located off the original dining room followed by a smaller breakfast room which served as the Office of the Bursar.

A wood-paneled game room located in the front left side was being used as a classroom.

After ascending the grand staircase to the second floor, the girls' dorms were located beyond a door on the left side of the hall, and the office of admissions was located under the staircase which led to the unoccupied third floor. Three classrooms and two faculty offices were located on the right side above the first floor drawing room. When I entered the admissions office, I was greeted by Dr. Preston Shoemaker, the Dean of Admissions, who invited me into his office. As we sat and talked about my background and interests, he provided me with an application for admission. He was very kind and made me feel very much at ease. Dr. Shoemaker also requested that I fill out the application and return it to him as soon as possible and that, on the basis of the interview (I didn't even know I was being interviewed!), he would recommend me for admission beginning in September of 1959. As I departed Florham that day, I was very impressed with the beauty of the campus, and both surprised and extremely pleased with my first experience at Fairleigh Dickinson. I then knew this was the college I wanted to attend!

Although I did receive a letter of admission to the University at the Florham Campus, I had learned of a special FDU program designed specifically to strengthen one's study skills. However, it was only offered through the Rutherford Campus. Since I thought such a program would be most beneficial, I then decided to enter the study skills program during the 1959-1960 academic year after which I transferred to the Florham Campus in the fall of 1960.

My Years as an Undergraduate Student at Florham in the College of Business (September 1960 – August 1963)

Gordon in yearbook

Gordon when chair

When I entered FDU Florham as a full-time student in 1960, some major changes in the campus were evident while some things remained the same as they had been in 1959. A dress code was strictly enforced and female students were required to wear skirts while all male students were required to wear jackets and ties to classes. Enrollment had increased to the point where more facilities were needed. The original Gate House still served as the Dean's residence; the Office of Admissions and the girls' dorm rooms were still located on the second floor of the mansion and, as I remember, the third floor was still unoccupied but was in the process of being renovated. Three classrooms and two faculty offices were still located on the second floor above the drawing room. The library was still located on the first floor and the Aeolian organ was still intact and in the process of being overhauled. The Bursar's Office was located at the end of the Great Hall on the left side and is now named the Sarah Sullivan Lounge. Office Services and the Campus Bookstore were located in the Mansion basement beneath the Drawing Room while the campus kitchen and cafeteria were located on the opposite side of the building where it opened into the courtyard. The Campus Bookstore and all University Food Services were operated by the University. In the early days, the campus housed programs in the College of Liberal Arts, the College of Business, the College of Education, and the College of Science & Engineering.

The original stable was being converted into the Science Building and housed some classrooms, four chemistry labs, three physics labs, three biology labs, as well as a typing room and a mechanical drawing lab for the College of Science & Engineering. The basement housed the facilities of the University Health Research Institute. Dr. William Smith was the Institute director while Mrs. Ruth Elsasser and Mrs. Doris Hubert served as laboratory technicians. The Institute was well known for its research in asbestosis, a type of lung cancer caused by inhaling asbestos fibers. It was also responsible for conducting nutrition studies with both animal and human foods.

The Playhouse was open and the main part of the building, originally an indoor tennis court, was used for convocations while the original swimming pool was open for student and faculty use. The main entrance to the building opened into a large hall with a cherry paneled lounge located on the left side while the pool, along with changing and showering facilities, was located on the right side of the hall. Continuing straight ahead led to the main part of the building which was now being used by the University for convocations and other large gatherings, as well as for the administration of final exams. The main part of the building did not have a basement. However, there was a small addition to the main building that did have a basement where a photographic darkroom was located and where a tunnel entrance was visible containing both electric cables as well as steam pipes that came from the powerhouse located behind the Orangerie.

The East Cottage housed the College of Business and included faculty offices and several classrooms while the West Cottage housed the College of Education and included faculty offices and several classrooms. [The cottages are located behind the Science Building.]

The Art and Music Departments were housed in a low wood-framed building located at the end of the parking lot behind the library building. This building may have originally been attached to the large greenhouse complex which was located behind the Orangerie. The greenhouse complex had been demolished and replaced by the parking lot and the outlines of the huge greenhouses can still be seen on the brick wall located around the parking lot. The low wood-framed building contained several classrooms, faculty offices for the Art and Music Departments, and also a large open art studio that served as an art exhibition hall. The men's dorms were located in a long narrow building that was later connected to the library building.

A cottage was located at the Danforth Gate entrance and served as the home of the resident engineer, Mr. McVeigh. After a number of years, the resident engineer position was eliminated when Mr. McVeigh retired and the building was converted to the University Health Center.

A high wall separated the tracks of the Lackawanna Railroad from the estate and sheds were attached to it that were being used for maintenance and storage. A barn was located on the opposite side of the driveway in front of the sheds and had been converted into several rooms on the ground floor, and was used mostly for music practice while the loft served as an art studio.

When I began my studies at Florham in the fall semester of 1960, I was enrolled in the College of Business with a major in business management and a minor in marketing. My advisor was Dr. Louis A. Rice, a former Dean of the Rutherford Campus. Most of my courses were offered during the daytime but I did have some evening classes. Dr. Paul Gillen, Director of Evening Programs, often came around to make sure the evening classes were meeting when scheduled.

President Peter Sammartino would visit the campus frequently each semester and would talk with students and sometimes enter a classroom and sit while the professor was conducting the class.

All freshman students were required to take Freshman Orientation, Health Education, and a course in Physical Education. In addition, all students were required to attend Convocation. Attendance was recorded and students in Freshman Orientation were required to write a summary and critique the presentation.

During my junior year as a business major, I decided to fulfill the science requirement by taking a two-semester course offered through the Chemistry Department. The course was taught by Dr. Norma Leeds, an adjunct professor who worked at Bell Labs in Murray Hill. The course was Science for the Technological Age. While the first semester concentrated on physical sciences, the second semester concentrated on the biological sciences, organic and biochemistry.

In high school, I had been very interested in geology and was enrolled in the scientific program which required taking Algebra I and II, Geometry, Trigonometry, Physics, and Chemistry. However, the program did not include a course in biology. Since my interest in geology had waned, and I enjoyed working in retail at that time, I then decided to major in business. After completing Science for the Technological Age, however, my interest in science was renewed and I decided to take Biology I and II as free electives during my senior year as a business major. Biology 201 was taught by Dr. Warren Ward and Biology 202 was taught by Dr. James Griffo. My interest in biology was really fired up and I then decided to continue as a biology major. However, I only had two courses left to complete requirements for the B.S. degree in Business Management. I made the decision to complete those courses and graduated with a B.S. degree in Business in October of 1963. I then transferred to the College of Arts & Sciences and began fulfilling requirements for a second B.S. degree in Biology.

While an undergraduate and graduate student at FDU, I enjoyed a good relationship with my professors and received a very excellent education and a thorough understanding of basic biological principles. I became more aware of my sound FDU education when I was in graduate classes at Rutgers with students from well-known colleges; I felt very comfortable knowing that I had a better knowledge of basic biological principles than most of them and I developed a good relationship with my professors at Rutgers.

Although all my professors and instructors at FDU were instrumental in providing me with a sound knowledge of biology, I am most indebted to Dr. Warren Ward and Dr. James Griffo, not only for their friendship, but also for their encouragement in the field of teaching and in their guidance and support in the development of my career as a Professor of Biology.

Dr. Ward asked if I would like to give a guest lecture but didn't give me a chance to respond! Since he knew I was interested in ferns, he told me to prepare a lecture and be ready the following week; before I began, Dr. Ward left the room but quietly entered the stockroom adjoining the lab and listened to my lecture; when finished, he entered

BIOLOGY DEPARTMENT
Dr. I. Huber, Mr. J. McMonis, Dr. W. Ward, Dr. F. Glenn,
Dr. R. Francoeur, Mr. R. G. Perry, Dr. F. Mullin, Mrs. R.
Elmore, Dr. P. Lenz.

81

the room and said he was pleased with my presentation; this was the beginning of my teaching career.

The following year I was appointed Laboratory Coordinator. Student enrollment was very high and the Biology Department offered 3-credit Botany and Zoology classes for non-science majors and 4-credit courses for biology majors; because of the large number of lab sections, I also served as a lab instructor, working closely with both Dr. Ward and Dr. Griffo.

I was appointed Visiting Lecturer in September 1966 and began studies for an M.S. Degree in Biology. That led to an appointment as Lecturer in September 1967, a position I held until 1976 when I became a full-time faculty member as Instructor; during this time, I taught an average of 18 contact hours, completed an M.S. degree in Biology (cum laude), and began working part-time toward a Ph.D. in Plant Pathology at Rutgers University.

As enrollments increased during the 1970s and into the mid 1980s, both Botany and Zoology were offered each spring and fall semester; as room in the Science Building was at a premium, all Botany courses were held in the service yard area; lectures were held in the Barn and the end of the sheds was converted into a botany lab. My office was relocated there. In the late 1980s, the Botany classes were returned to the Science Building in room S-3 with my office in S-3A.

After earning my Ph.D degree at Rutgers in 1981, I was awarded tenure and promoted to Assistant Professor and, in 1987, promoted to Associate Professor. I was appointed chairman of the Department of Biological & Allied Health Sciences beginning in July 1996 and served as Chairman until 2002.

Campus Faculty

When the campus opened for classes in the fall of 1958, the professorial staff numbered eight full-time faculty and twenty part-time evening faculty. By the 1961 academic year, the full-time faculty had grown to sixty-nine and the evening faculty to 100. By 1966-67, the full-time faculty had grown to seventy-nine.

The campus and its students were fortunate to enjoy the stability of a faculty with minimal turnover, people who came soon after the campus' founding and participated in the growth and development of the education program and the facilities. Faculty throughout the academic disciplines came to know each other well, both through working together on committees and informal social contact. They gathered at each other's home or at campus events. Chemists, mathematicians, psychologists, literature professors, and others became personal friends. They knew their colleagues and the students they shared as individuals.

An important reason for these associations was the fact that most lived in communities near the campus, the result of Dean Samuel Pratt's insistence when faculty were hired. New faculty began to resist this requirement, in great part because the development of the Florham Park–Madison area brought a great increase in housing costs and raised the cost of home purchases beyond the range of faculty salaries.

As the student residential population grew and more lived on campus and in apartments in the community, opportunites for faculty-student socialization increased. Students were invited to faculty homes and faculty to student gatherings, such as poetry readings. They also collaborated on academic and creative projects. A number of these partnerships grew into lifelong friendships.

Two individuals played special roles in the development of the campus—Walter Savage, in English, in the liberal arts, and Malcolm Sturchio, a chemist, in the sciences. Both had been teaching on other University campuses before they were asked to help create an entirely new educational entity.

Walter T. Savage

Walter T. Savage, as one of the initial eight full-time faculty, lectured on literature to the entire student body in what had been the Twombly drawing room, now an assembly hall. As part of his administrative assignment, he interviewed and hired additional faculty in the humanities and social sciences. He helped provide books for the new library by visiting used book stores in Philidelphia, where he had gone to graduate school, and literally purchasing entire shelves of books.

A charismatic man, full of outgoing enthusiasm, energy, and playful wit, Savage—through his example and his personality—did much to create a campus culture in the example he set and in the people he attracted to the faculty. As a raconteur, he entertained students in classrooms, colleagues at meetings and lunch tables, and staff members in the offices he visited frequently, often forgetting his briefcase. People looked forward to his presence.

He served as an information historian of the Twomblys and their half-century presence at Florham, often leading tours of the campus and giving public lectures on the legacy of the family, the architecture, and the grounds.

Savage was one of the most popular professors at FDU, and his dedication was recognized in the many awards he received during his career. He was the recipient of the Alumni Great Teacher Award, the University's Distinguished Faculty Award for Service, and was named to FDU's Heritage Hall for his instrumental role in the development of the University. He also was awarded an honorary doctor of humane letters degree from FDU in 1984, and later received an honorary doctor of humanities degree from Monmouth University in 1992.

Twice in his career at the University—1966-67 and 1984-85—he was chosen to serve as acting dean of Wroxton College in Oxfordshire, England. The diary of his experiences was collected into a book titled *Walter Savage's Wroxton Journals*. The faculty lounge at Wroxton is named for him.

Savage also served as Acting President of the University in 1982-83. After his retirement from teaching, he devoted much of his time to the boards of several organizations, including the Friends of Florham, a group of volunteers who raise funds to restore the Mansion and the gardens to their state during the Twombly era.

Malcolm Sturchio

Mal Struchio joined the University in 1952 as a very young man and served in many capacities in a career that lasted fifty-seven years. Most of those years he was a professor of chemistry and science education, teaching tens of thousands of chemistry students and trained thousands more science teachers.

Beyond the classroom, during his long career, Sturchio directed the admissions department, served as acting dean of two colleges, chaired two academic departments, administered the continuing education program, created programs for high school science students, and served on just about every departmental, college, campus and University committee at one time or another.

In light of his knowledge of the sciences and his administrative experience, he was considered an ideal person to build a science facility and recruit a science faculty for the University's newest campus. He was also held in high regard by Peter Sammartino. Sturchio, in the decades that followed, more than justified the trust the University president had placed in him.

Together with two friends and colleagues, he wrote the textbook *Chemistry: Principles and Concepts* (1966), and also published other works on laboratory techniques in general chemistry and articles on chemical education. He extended his influence to science education in New Jersey and nationally, having led the NJ State Science Day and NJ Science League for decades, and held leadership positions in the NJ Science Teachers Association, the NJ Science Supervisors Association, and the NJ Science Education Leadership Association, as well as the National Science Teachers Association.

Sturchio also played an important role in international relations in chemistry and education, particularly in his close relationship to the Korean chemists community and involvement in introducing modern science curricula to Korea following an appointment as Senior Fulbright Scholar at Seoul National University in 1965-66. He also served as science education advisor to the Korean Ministry of Education (1967-68) and as a member of the ROK- US Science Council, as well as a consultant to the Regional Center for Science and Mathematics, South East Asia Ministers of Education Secretariat (SEAMES) in the late 1960s and early 1970s.

In recognition of his long dedication to Korean-American educational exchange, he received honorary doctorates from both Kyung Hee University (1971) and Kyungnam University (1989). He also received the FDU Distinguished Faculty Award for Service in 1995, and a Doctor of Humane Letters degree from the University in 1998.

Faculty Dinners and Picnics

In addition to their off-campus friendships and gatherings, faculty members frequently gathered on campus for dinners and picnics. Occasionally, the meals were formal, but more often they were casual and pot luck, those attending each bringing a dish to be shared. Spouses, partners, and sometimes children attended.

Faculty, staff members, and friends gather on the Mansion Portico

Families enjoying a spring picnic on the campus grounds

The Faculty Dining Room

Harry Keyishian, Professor of English Emeritus

When I arrived at Fairleigh Dickinson University in 1965, the first spot I cultivated was the Faculty Dining Room. Located in the present Provost's office, it was an elegant establishment with white tablecloths, attractive decor, and a companionable staff. I don't recall how the food was, but more to the point, it was the place of resort and conversation for faculty and their guests, an on-site club at which newcomers could feel welcome, get to know colleagues, and come to understand the culture of the institution they were joining.

The Faculty Dining Room was a place for relaxed conversation, discussion, and exchange of ideas. It was also the spot to hear or tell jokes, keep an eye on rivals, gossip, flirt, or whatever else one had a mind to. Friendships could be formed and cultivated, and momentous schemes hatched and developed. Though departmental colleagues might tend to sit together, initially, there were also plentiful opportunities to meet faculty and staff from other departments.

Sam and Lois Pratt were constant presences there, deeply into any and all discussions. They were entirely in their element exchanging ideas, sharing current enthusiasms, and debating current issues. Faculty and administrators did not, as they have on occasion since, seem breeds apart, involved in incompatible activities, but, rather, partners in the academic enterprise.

It was a policy strictly held to, however, that the Dean and the Professor of Sociology did not sit together at lunch, so that there would never be a single "official" location in the dining room.

(I recall they once, by accident, found themselves seated at the same table, and treated the event like a major scandal, never to be repeated.)

Gorham Munson

Traffic was fairly constant in the dining room, as faculty and staff came and went with the change of classes, but there was also "down" time, when the place was largely empty and one could relax with a cup of coffee alone or with a friend. I had the good fortune for a full year to share a lunch table twice a week with editor and biographer Gorham Munson, a man deeply involved in the culture of the 1920s, friend and editor of Hart Crane, and intimate of many of his contemporaries. Having Gorham to myself for a couple of hours a week, I soaked up all I could about the period, both literary and trivial, so that when the opportunity came to write a book about another figure of the 1920s, I plunged ahead with a confidence born of those conversations.

The lunchroom was shut down shortly after Sam left the University. This was partly due to costs, partly to the then-faddish notion that faculty should be dispersed among students rather than clustering together. I suspect, too, that a failure to appreciate the value of community and intellectual exchange also lay behind it—a costly failure because, in my view, nothing comparable ever replaced that dining room—not even its electronic successor, the e-mail bulletin board (which Sam, in fact, anticipated). I'll always remain grateful to Sam Pratt for maintaining a location where intellectual exchange, the heartbeat of any academic institution, was cultivated and honored.

THE ARTS ON CAMPUS

This article, co-written in 1962 by Kalliope (Poppy) Decavalles for Lois Pratt's journal *University Woman* expresses Samuel Pratt's philosophy of the role of the arts in education and the artistic activities he brought to the campus in its early years.

A central purpose of a university's education is the development of creative abilities. Many educational institutions in the United States have started a campaign to obtain along with their curriculum program a Cultural and Artistic Life. To pioneer in developing new trends in women's education, the Madison campus of Fairleigh Dickinson University is extending its activity in the development of a serious art program.

"An aesthetic life" states Dr. Samuel Pratt, Dean of the Madison campus, "has many dimensions varying from basic personal behavior to the creation of great masterpieces. Not many are capable of masterpieces but we are all more than capable of an aesthetic life in its other dimensions. We can express it, among other ways, in our study and appreciation of art forms, the building of a cultural library at home, museum membership and use, conversation, quiet periods of reflection, and in our manners and dress."

This educational philosophy is expressed in many ways at Fairleigh Dickinson University, such as in the concern with the development of both a strong liberal arts curricular program for all students and a student life cultural program open to all, through an emphasis on concerts, art exhib-

"Arms and the Man" production, 1961

its, drama and similar programs, the steady efforts to build a great collection of art, the design of buildings and the selection and care of furnishings, and in the concern for personal grace from the motto "Fortiter et Suavitar" [Strongly and Gently] to dress.

All phases of arts are represented and performed at the Madison campus of Fairleigh Dickinson University, thus giving the opportunity to students and the community to enjoy fine programs. The University sponsors programs produced by noted groups in the world of arts.

A highlight of the University's efforts toward the development of creative abilities is the Student Arts Festival. The idea underlying the Festival is that the arts play a significant role in building the imaginative and creative powers of individuals. As such, the Festival is part of the University program designed to prepare students for a life-long role in the arts as creators, collectors, members of audiences, and conversationalists.

The Student Arts Festival has a further objective of providing a significant outlet to students where they may gain experience through performance. From the point of view of the individual participant, one of the important objectives is the great self-satisfaction that the individual can find in doing something creative, whether in painting, dance music, writing, or drama. Finally, through seeing performances, students not now participating may come to realize the great personal values that can be obtained through an active life in the arts.

The student's publication "dele arti," a magazine published and staffed by the students of this campus,

International artists, 1961

91

is very pertinent to the entire festival. The publication's main purposes are: to give the student an opportunity to exhibit and receive recognition of his work and to enable the students to publish a superior magazine.

The campus has also inaugurated an experimental international art program. This pilot project, called the International Artists Summer Seminar, evolved from two basic premises held by the University—the education of foreign persons and of U.S. citizens about other countries, and concern with the general development of culture and individual growth in the arts. It has proved to be such a rewarding and stimulating experience for the international artists and those who joined them, that it will be enlarged this summer.

A most interesting feature of the Seminar is the Art Workshop which is open to the public. These participants work at least 10 hours per week under the supervision of international artists. They also join in on many of the informal lectures and social functions. With art as link, the cultural differences and language barriers prove to be of little importance. What develops is an exciting stimulus for all artists in relation to this work and a camaraderie so unbelievable and simple as to again bring truth to the words that art is a universal language.

At the Madison campus, a student in the Fine Arts program prepares for a number of professional fields. In combining intensive studies in all of the Fine Arts—Art, Drama, Dance, and Music—with minors selected from Business Management, Education, Sociology, Literature, Psychology, Philosophy, and Languages, the student will obtain a wide background. A major like this will lead the student toward graduate specialization in any of the Fine Arts. He will also be suited for a career in the applied arts, such as production, advertising, publishing, or interior decorating; public relations in the arts, music, or theater industries; teacher education; management of museums, art centers, and cultural associations; youth educational direction in public and private youth centers; criticism; and community cultural leadership. The courses will also fulfill the need of students seeking a purely aesthetic education.

WOMEN'S EDUCATION

Students enrolled at colleges and universities in the 1950s were disproportionately male. A concerted effort was made at the Madison campus to increase the enrollment of women and to provide encouragement and opportunities for women students to aspire, to develop, and to lead.

Dean Pratt framed the issue in a 1963 campus publication on *Women's Activities*:

One of the fundamental features of modern life is the drastically altered and expanded role expected of women. The expectation concerning educated women in the United States is that they are capable of leadership performance in a career, family, citizenship, moral associations, curtural life, and social and recreational activities. While such a six-sided woman is a rarity, it is the model toward which young college women are being asked to strive.

University Woman magazine published between 1962 and 1965 was designed to be a reflective documentation of both opportunities and problems. Each issue was organized around a different theme. Several campus conferences were organized around this theme. The magazine provided an opportunity for women students to write articles for publication based on serious research, interviews, poetry, and historical analysis, as well as to publish their artwork and photography. The publication received national exposure.

The themes included "The Educating of the Modern Woman," "Beauty and the Creative Woman," "The Creative Woman in Science," "Women of New Jersey," and "The Ills of Modern Women."

FAMOUS VISITORS

Well-known writers, artists, and political figures visited the campus during its initial years. They included the artist Elaine de Kooning; the novelist, playwright, poet, literary critic, and psychotherapist Paul Goodman; political figures Barry Goldwater and Robert F. Kennedy; and the novelist and story writer Shirley Jackson and her husband, the literary critic Stanley Edgar Hyman.

Barry Goldwater, 1961

Robert F. Kennedy, 1963

The Jackson visit was described in Ruth Franklin's biography, *Shirley Jackson: A Rather Haunted Life,* with Jackson's lecture and reading among her first after a mental breakdown:

> ... she had to sit through Stanley's event, a three-hour panel discussion. "then a coffee hour with the students (no coffee for me, thanks) and then a cocktail party (that they didn't take away from me, thank heaven)." Her hosts took her and Stanley out to dinner at a fancy restaurant, where she suffered paroxysms of guilt when she was unable to eat the expensive steak that was ordered for her. Somehow she made it through her own lecture, before an audience of five hundred, with Stanley in the front row, ready to escort her out if necessary.

Lois and Samuel Pratt waving goodbye

www.ingramcontent.com/pod-product-compliance
Lightning Source LLC
Chambersburg PA
CBHW042011090426

42811CB00015B/1617